tiime

TOGETHER IN MINISTRY EVERYDAY

52 Devotions

M. KENT MILLARD, General Editor

Abingdon Press
Nashville

TOGETHER IN MINISTRY EVERYDAY: 52 DEVOTIONS

This book is printed on acid-free, recycled paper.

08 09 10 11 12 13 14 15 16 17 – 10 9 8 7 6 5 4 3 2 1

MANUFACTURED IN THE UNITED STATES OF AMERICA

Contents

Go Fish! Series

"As Jesus walked by the Sea of Galilee, he saw two brothers, Simon, who is called Peter, and Andrew his brother, casting a net into the sea—for they were fishermen. And he said to them 'Follow me and I will make you fish for people.' Immediately, they left their nets and followed him." Matthew 4:18-20

Go Fish! consists of forty playing cards with different brightly colored fish (pink, red, orange, purple, brown, green, blue, yellow, white, or gray) on each individual card. The goal is to get a set of four cards of the same color fish and lay them down in front of you. The person who gets the most sets of same-colored fish is the winner of the game.

A player will ask other players if they have a certain color fish card in their hand and if they do, they have to surrender it to the person requesting it. If they don't have it they will say GO FISH! and the player requesting the card will have to draw a card from the central stack.

Many young children love to play this game, and I have played it for hours with my young grandchildren. The principle of the game is simple. If you cannot get the card you need from another player you have to GO FISH! which means you have to reach out and hope to draw the card you need.

The GO FISH! SERIES is about encouraging followers of Jesus to "GO FISH" which means to reach out to the people in their communities in compassionate, loving ways so that people without any current interest in following Jesus might want to come and become a part of a particular faith community.

Jesus practiced the same principle when he called the brothers Peter and Andrew to become his first followers. Peter and Andrew were fishermen on the Sea of Galilee, which means that they would get in their boat each day, go out to the deep part of the lake, throw out their nets, and hopefully pull in a catch of fish.

Peter and Andrew did not sit in their boat near the shore and wait for the fish to come and jump into their boat. They knew that they had to go out to the deep water in order to catch the fish and bring them into their boat. They had to reach out to catch the fish; the fish wouldn't automatically come to them. They had to GO FISH!

In a similar way, congregations need to go out into their neighborhoods and communities in loving and serving ways if they want to invite more persons to become followers of Jesus who make a positive difference in the world. Congregational leaders need to learn how to GO FISH! in their communities.

Just as we do not expect fish to come and simply jump into a boat because it is there, we cannot expect that somehow people will simply come and jump into our congregations because we are there.

The first handbook, workbook, and DVD of the GO FISH! series encourages congregations to focus on outreach ministries that meet the pressing needs of people in their own communities.

Future emphases for the GO FISH! series will offer effective ways of following up with first-time visitors, how to share faith personally in an authentic and meaningful way, how to reach new persons through children and family ministries, how to use various public media outlets in reaching our communities, and how to develop a climate of hospitality for persons who are not yet a part of a congregation.

Each title of the series is written by a practicing local pastor or lay leader in a congregation that is effectively reaching out and leading people to become followers of Jesus Christ.

Our goal is not simply to enable congregations to grow in participation and membership. Our goal is that congregations will become vital centers of loving service for the spiritual and personal needs of the people of their communities so that the world will be transformed into a compassionate, just, inclusive, and Christ-like community.

The ultimate goal of the GO FISH! series is to be used by God for the transformation of the people in our communities from fear to faith, from complacency to compassion, and from greed to generosity. Our hope is that more and more people will be become followers of Jesus, who is still at work in transforming and redeeming our world.

Acknowledgements

We are indebted to many people at St. Luke's United Methodist Church who did the "heavy lifting" in helping our congregation to become a more outward-focused congregation.

We are especially indebted to the leadership team who first led us to a new vision of "being transformed by God so God could use us to transform the world into a compassionate, just, inclusive, and Christ-like community."

Then we are indebted to the Together in Ministry Everyday task force who prayed, reflected, organized, and encouraged the whole congregation to become outward-focused in all of our ministry areas. They helped us to see that this was not simply one other program of our congregation, but a change of our church culture so we are mindful of the impact and responsibility we have as Christians on and towards our local and global community.

We are also indebted to all the members and friends of our congregation who actually gave more of their T.I.M.E. to serve people in need in our congregation and community and beyond. Literally hundreds of persons are giving more of their time, talent, and treasure in loving and serving hundreds of other people in the name of Jesus Christ, and everyone is being blessed in the process. The one comment we have heard over and over again is, "I received far more than I gave." Our motivation for caring for others is not so that we will be blessed, but the reality is that when we unselfishly share our lives and love with others we cannot help but be blessed.

Most of all we want to give the glory to God, who inspires, prods, challenges, supports, and blesses all those who seek to carry out Jesus' command to "tend my sheep."

Kent Millard and Lori Crantford
June 2008

God Encounters

Why would anyone want to read another devotional guide?

That is the question someone asked me when we invited members of our congregation to write down their stories and experiences about our outward-focused ministries. We asked persons in our congregation to share an experience of reaching out to care for someone either within or beyond our congregation and how they felt the spirit of God working through them in ways they could not have anticipated.

But why would other people want to know about these God-experiences? As I pondered this thoughtful question these responses came to mind.

First, we believe that God is present and around us at every moment of our lives—as real as the air we breathe. We are surrounded by the air that gives us life, but we usually take it for granted and rarely become aware and appreciative of the sustainable air we breathe. In a similar way, we are surrounded by the living Spirit of God who gives and sustains our lives, but we often take God's presence for granted as well.

A devotional guide is simply an invitation to slow down and become aware and appreciative of the presence of God around us. When we slow down and reflect on a passage of Scripture and read about the real experience of another person who has tried to respond to the call of God, we might become inspired to listen for the voice of God in our own lives and respond to God's call to us.

The truth about life is that the Living Christ is always present around us and within us, but the question is: Are we present? Are we present, attentive, aware, and listening for the call of God in our lives to love and serve in the name of Christ, or are we so consumed with our own agendas, thoughts, and concerns that there is no way for God to get a thought in edgewise?

I confess that sometimes I am so consumed with my own thoughts, plans, and ideas that I know God has a hard time getting my attention and leading me in God's ways. Sometimes it seems that my mind is a constant stream of thinking, with one thought following the other in rapid succession.

I once read that God comes in the space between thoughts, and when there is no space between our thoughts, it is difficult for us to hear the "still, small voice of God" within us. Perhaps that is also why the Psalmist wrote: "Be still and know that I am God" (Psalm 46:10).

My own experience is that when I slow down on a regular basis, take a few deep breaths, sit in silence for a few minutes, ponder some verses of Scripture and a reflect on an experience of a fellow follower of Jesus, I am inspired to become available to hear the whispers and nudgings of God in my own life.

I also find it helpful to keep a prayer journal where I write down my thoughts and prayers to God following this time of silence and reflection. Frequently, something I read in Scripture or from another person stimulates my own spirit, giving me guidance for my life that day. I also often discover that when I meditate on a verse of Scripture I discover that it is exactly the guidance I needed for that day.

A few years ago, I received a certain honor and I was feeling pretty proud of myself. Then my devotional guide for the next day quoted the passage where Paul wrote these words: "I say to everyone among you not to think of yourself more highly than you ought to think" (Romans 12:3).

It seemed that those words were written just for me for that moment in my life. I was thinking too highly of myself, and Paul reminded me of the danger of ego and pride. I am always amazed how certain words of Scripture frequently come to me at just the time I need them . . . but I don't discover them unless I take time for Scripture reading, reflection, and prayer.

God Encounters

My first answer to this question about why another devotional guide is needed is that perhaps this guide will encourage people who have a natural tendency to be active in service to be still and listen for God's guidance in their lives as they go into the world to serve.

A second reason for this devotional guide is to remind us that our motivation for loving service in the name of Christ comes from God and not from our desire for recognition or praise for doing good in the world.

I have discovered that my ego is so strong that sometimes I can do the right thing for the wrong reason. When I do something good for another person and then want thanks, recognition, or praise for doing it, I know I am doing it for the wrong reason. I am doing it to stroke my ego. Acts of mercy done for the wrong reason leave a bad taste in the mouth of God and in the mouths of those who are served.

In meditation I find myself asking if a certain action is coming out of my soul or out of my ego. I once read that E. G. O. simply means "Edging God Out." I realize that my ego is always trying to edge God out of life and take over the controls. I also know that when I acknowledge that something is coming out of my ego, my ego loses its power for a moment, and the same action can be performed from the spirit of God within me rather than from a desire for recognition or praise. A devotional guide like this helps us check our motives. It gives God a chance to help us recognize when we are motivated by the Spirit of God or our egos.

Finally, a third reason for this devotional guide is to share the authentic experiences of people who have allowed themselves to be used by God for the loving service of others. A bishop once came to visit the congregation I was serving. After the service I was eager to talk with him and tell him all the great things happening in our congregation. However, he didn't seem much interested in talking with me. He kept turning his attention to various lay people in our congregation and getting all of his information about our congregation from them.

At first, I was a little miffed. Then I realized that he was a very wise man. I had a vested interest in seeking to impress him with the ministries of our church because he was my boss and I wanted to make a good impression. However, he was wise enough to know that the lay persons in our congregation might be more honest and frank about the strengths and weaknesses of our congregation without the same vested interest that I had.

In a similar way, I am tempted to try to impress others with the outward-focus ministries of our congregation, but the lay members and others who wrote for this book may not have the same agenda. Consequently, they can share with you honestly about the joys and challenges of being an outward-focused congregation and their authentic experiences and surprises of seeking to "tend the sheep" of God.

My prayer is that this devotional guide will be an occasion for God-encounters, will help you recognize when you are acting in response to your soul or your ego, and will inspire you serve others in the name of Jesus Christ. May you and your congregation join Together in Ministry Everyday so that God will be praised and people will be loved, served, and transformed.

Grace and Peace,

Kent Millard

TOGETHER IN MINISTRY EVERYDAY

52 Devotions

1
A Mother's Strength

By Jackie Reed

"O, my strength, I will sing praises to you, for you, O God, are my fortress, the God who shows me steadfast love" (Psalm 59:17).

God loves me, comforts me, and gives me strength.

Today, I am reflecting on how my world changed nine years ago when our son, Greg, did not return home from a night out with friends. We reported Greg missing and prayed for his safe return. On a September day, Greg's remains were found. After months of praying for his safe return, I thought God had let me down. My grief was so overwhelming; I could not believe our son was gone. How could this happen to Greg? To our family? My husband and I had just attended a Billy Graham rally. We had prayed for healing and guidance for Greg and an end to his suffering with severe depression.

God answered our prayers, but not the way I had expected. Greg is no longer suffering with depression, nor with the heartaches of this life that weighed so heavily on his shoulders. I wanted him back and I screamed to God to give him back to me. I was so lost and hopeless. I prayed that God would take me, too. I did not have the strength within to keep going. One day I felt, more than heard, God's message: "You are needed here. You are stronger. Your husband and daughter need you to love and support them through their own grief." I responded in praying, "Please, Lord, give me comfort and the strength to live. Where and what do you want me to do?"

God's answer came five years later while I was attending a Stephen Ministry meeting at St. Luke's, my home church. Someone spoke to our group about needing help preparing meals for Outreach, Inc., a ministry serving homeless and at-risk youth. Before I knew it, God shot my hand up!

On the way home I prayed, asking if this is where God wanted me. Was Outreach my place to serve? I contacted Outreach and learned that they were in the process of relocating two blocks from where we last knocked on doors and put up flyers for our missing Greg, the same day his remains were discovered. I received my answer from God.

Four years later, I am still providing meals for Outreach youth, with financial help from members of St. Luke's. When Greg was missing I prayed for someone to take care of Greg, to feed him, give him shelter, and guide him back home to us. God has given me the blessing of loving these young people. Each and every time I receive a hug from a youth, I am receiving a hug from Greg. God has blessed me with strength and comfort each and every day. Outreach has allowed me to heal and turn my grief and loss into serving our Lord, one meal at a time.

God, we pray for all those who have lost loved ones. We know our loved ones are at peace with you. May we find your peace here on earth as we love them and let them go. Show us where you would have us serve and bring us healing, amen.

2
Answering the Call

By Ron Sinicki

"I. . . beg you to lead a life worthy of the calling to which you have been called" (Ephesians 4:1).

What does it really mean to be a Christian? I used to be what I call a "check-the-box Christian." Eight years of parochial school? Check! Go to church every week? Check! Pray every night? Check! I was doing all the right things—checking all the right boxes.

In recent years, however, I started to realize that for me those things weren't enough—it was time to start "walking the walk" and putting my faith into action. I kept reading in the bulletin about a group called Stephen Ministry, a one-on-one Christian-based crisis ministry. For over a year, I came up with some pretty creative reasons why I was ignoring that little voice in my ear saying "Why don't you check into it?"

It all came to a head one July Sunday several years ago when Adolph Hansen was preaching. To go with his sermon, inside each bulletin was a small card with a paraphrase of Ephesians 4:1, "I am inviting you to lead a life worthy of your call." Could there be any clearer sign that it was time to get off the couch and do something? The next day I enrolled to be a Stephen Minister, making a promise to walk as a Christian friend with a total stranger who was going through a difficult time in his life. Someone who would listen, not judge, and just be there when needed.

For nearly the next two years I was matched with my "care receiver." He was going through a rough stretch in his life at the time, and we met once a week to talk about whatever was on his mind that day. Some days it was his personal situation, some days it was the Colts' latest win or loss, thoughts about God, the weather, music, and many other topics. We would end each meeting with a prayer, usually with me leading and praying for our families and whatever he wanted to pray for that day. I think it was comforting to him to know there was someone out there willing to pray for him and his situation.

What did I get out of that experience? I'm quite sure I benefited more from our time together than he did. There is an overwhelming feeling of joy that comes with helping someone in need, and playing an oh-so-small part in his journey to a better place. What could be better than that? We have a saying in Stephen Ministry: "We are the care giver, and God is the *cure* giver." That's absolutely true.

I still have the small card from that July sermon years ago with the verse from St. Paul on it taped up at my desk at work. It's my daily reminder that one person can make a difference if we're willing to try.

God our Father, thank you for helping me to see beyond myself. Help me to always be a faithful servant and lead a life worthy of my calling, amen.

3
Some People Are Like That

By Kathy Dalton

"Whatever you do, in word or deed, do everything in the name of the Lord Jesus" (Colossians 3:17).

One of my best friends persuaded me to go on my first mission trip in April. While growing up, my church youth group was always doing mission work. But as an adult, this type of trip never seemed to fit into my agenda. Following Hurricane Katrina, when my husband became deeply involved with the Seashore District Volunteer Center in D'Iberville, Mississippi and was looking for volunteers for the eight-week project, my friend Margaret convinced me this was "our time." Our children were now grown and out from under our wings, and I could find no other excuses for not going. We packed up the car and set out on our eight-hundred-mile journey to the Mississippi Gulf Coast. We drove till dark, solved all the world's problems in just a few short hours, and stopped for the night.

The next morning was Easter, and while enjoying our breakfast, we were joined by a delightful set of grandparents who had their two young grandchildren in tow. We shared our travel stories. They were headed across the state to a big family Easter celebration. We were headed to Mississippi to assist hurricane victims. All four of them were deeply engrossed in our story and where we were going. When we parted, they thanked us for volunteering our time to help the hurricane victims. We thanked them for being such wonderful breakfast companions on Easter morning. They were like family, and our paths had only crossed for thirty minutes! Some people are like that. We continued on our journey, four hundred miles to go. We listened to an Easter message on the radio and then listened to Michael W. Smith's *Worship* album over and over. It was an Easter Sunday we will always remember.

Aside from the amazing experiences one gains from going on a mission trip, and anyone who has ever been on a mission trip knows what these are, one of our fifteen roommates was the highlight of my trip. Vickie was a pastor from the Chicago area and she was unlike anyone I had ever met. To put it simply, she was angelic, and we all became fast friends. She was like family, and we had only known her for thirty minutes! Some people are like that. After working side by side with Vickie, and dozens of other volunteers for a week, I told Margaret on our way home that my goal in life was to become more "Vickie-like." She was as close to "God-like" as a person could get. I went to Mississippi to help others, but came away helping myself. I owe a lot to Vickie for showing me the way, just by being herself. Some people are like that.

Dear God, thank you for sending special people into our lives who will help steer us in the right direction. Help us to become more like you with each passing day, amen.

4
Better Together

By Stan Abell and Joshua Mbithi

"Two are better than one, because they have a good reward for their toil. For if they fall, one will lift up the other; but woe to one who is alone and falls and does not have another to help. Again, if two lie together, they keep warm; but how can one keep warm alone? And though one might prevail against another, two will withstand one. A threefold cord is not quickly broken"

(Ecclesiastes 4:9-12).

"We're one, but we're not the same, we get to carry each other."

—"One," by U2

My friend Joshua Mbithi said what I think most of us value as true, but often have a hard time embracing. He said, "God's timing is the best." In my own life I have found this simple idea to be true but all too difficult to follow. I like things to happen on my schedule—when I think things should or should not happen. Many of us feel much more comfortable when we have complete control over every aspect of our lives, including our relationships, our work, and our families. However, in meeting Joshua Mbithi, his wife Miriam, and the HIV-infected and affected orphans they serve every day, I'm reminded that when I take my watch off and put God's on, and when I let go of control and allow God to use me for God's purposes, not mine, lives are richly blessed— most of all mine.

One summer, several of us went to Kenya to film a documentary on the AIDS crisis there. I was there to film, to tell a story; I had an agenda. I was quite confident that my work was going to help change lives. Our team's work was going to make a difference in the lives of many Kenyans. Yes, we did complete the film. Yes, many good things have happened as a result, but the truth of the matter is that the lives most changed have been our own. This has occurred because of a rich partnership with Joshua. So often we think of outreach work as ministry *for* instead of ministry *with*. Our paradigm is often what we can *do* for *those* people. Joshua has shown me what happens when, together, we work towards God's purposes.

Joshua stated it very simply, "You have been used by God to empower us, and God has used us to empower the children." The only way this was possible was by both of us being patient, trusting that God was at work in the middle of this, and trusting in each other. In allowing time for God to go to work, a new orphanage has been built by Kenyans to serve the most vulnerable of vulnerable victims of this devastating pandemic—children. After three years of dreaming and praying, a home was built to care for these precious children who have been abandoned.

All of this is incredibly humbling. As Joshua and I sat together, it occurred to both of us just how richly these children have blessed both of our lives. Alone, neither one of us could have made these things happen. Together, in partnership, we have created a shared blessing—a blessing we both give and receive. Joshua is convinced that God ordained the time of our meeting: "It was God's time for us to meet." I too believe it was God's time, and thank God for the blessing of this relationship.

Gracious God, when we allow you to be our guide in our work with others, when we put aside our agendas and adopt yours, we are so richly blessed. Amen.

5
Big John

By Max Hill

"Do not judge, so that you may not be judged" (Matthew 7:1).

His name is John—Big John. He weighs over three hundred pounds and sports a Mohawk haircut. John lives alone in a one-room, cluttered apartment close to Fletcher Place Community Center near inner-city Indianapolis. On disability, he depends upon Fletcher Place to provide breakfast, some dinners, and other food from the Community Pantry. He has faced many problems in his life: brushes with the law, drug use, and estrangement from his family.

Three years ago I met John when he enrolled in an adult literacy class I was helping teach at Fletcher Place. I must admit my first reactions to John were not very positive. As most of us do, I concentrated on his external appearance and demeanor and drew my own conclusion. Then an amazing thing happened. I soon discovered John is really quite a character; maybe rough on the outside, but very loving on the inside.

Despite living on a small disability check, John is quite generous and deeply concerned with helping others meet their needs. I have been most impressed by his strong faith and belief in God. His favorite Bible passage is Acts 2:38: "Repent, and be baptized every one of you in the name of Jesus Christ so that your sins may be forgiven, and you will receive the gift of the Holy Spirit."

Together each one of us has grown. Through his literacy training, John has developed improved skills in reading and writing and also gained a stronger sense of self-esteem. He recently graduated from our three-year literacy program and now wants to pursue his GED.

I have been reminded to stop making personal judgments by just looking at someone's "book cover." Underneath the skin of each of us, God has planted a loving soul. That is the message I am receiving from my friend, Big John.

Dear Lord, so often, when we look at other humans, we tend to focus on how they look or what they wear or their status in life. May we strive more to remember that every person is your beloved creation. Help us to look below the external surface and seek the hidden glory all of us possess. Amen.

6
Buddy

By Bill Johnson

"I was naked and you gave me clothing, I was sick and you took care of me, I was in prison and you visited me" (Matthew 25:36).

A group of seminarians, at the school where I am working on a Master of Divinity degree, started leading morning worship at a nearby state prison. Along with four other students, we rotate a preaching schedule at a men's prison on Sunday mornings. It was a great opportunity to practice preaching while in seminary, but more importantly I saw it as a way to witness about the love of God in Christ Jesus to the men who attend the service.

After a short time, a real community feeling started to form among the prisoners. Each worship service allowed a time for testimony, where some would share their struggles, concerns, and the spiritual victories both large and small. During one service, a prisoner announced that he had received word that his sentence was about over and he would be leaving in a couple of weeks. Buddy was an imposing feature of a man. He was in his early fifties, full head of thick white hair, and well-built. He could clearly handle any situation. Buddy was one tough guy. So I was surprised as he stood to speak. His head was slightly bowed and all I could see was his white hair. His voice was low and as he spoke he held everyone's attention. Buddy fought to control his emotions and his quivering voice as he told us how concerned he had been about living on his own. Could he make it "out there?" Would he end up in prison again? It was a sentiment shared by most prisoners.

Then Buddy cleared his throat and spoke with more assurance, saying he now felt confident that he was going to be "okay." A church had agreed to help him transition into life outside prison. Buddy told of a small group from a church that was helping him set goals, find a safe place to live, and find a job. Most importantly to Buddy, they wanted him to attend their church. His support team from church was even doing a Bible study with him. As tears were rolling down his cheeks, Buddy said that before he was sent to prison, he didn't care about anyone, so he didn't care if he hurt anyone or stole someone's property. If he wanted something, he decided to take it. That's why he was in prison, he explained. As he cleared his throat again, Buddy stood tall and looked around at each of his fellow prisoners and said that the real problem was that he didn't love himself. But things were different now, because a small group of people loved him.

Buddy said, "A strange thing happened; I started to love myself. And then I started to care about other people. Ya see, I didn't care about myself so it was easy not to care about anyone else or what they owned. But now I see things different. Jesus has showed me what true love is through my new church family." Then he said, "Don't give up! God has some people who will love you, too. Ya just have to be willin' to try to let folks in."

From that worship service on, I realized that I was no longer "practicing" for some future parish. This was church. God wants to reach everyone with the message of unconditional love and acceptance. One church understood, and I am so grateful that they had the courage to love Buddy.

Oh God, we pray for all persons in prison and for those who visit them, love them, and help them re-enter their community. In Christ's name, amen.

7
Construction Ministries

By Kathy Minx

"Just then some men came, carrying a paralyzed man on a bed. They were trying to bring him in and lay him before Jesus" (Luke 5:18).

Three years ago, I was on the Board of Directors of CICOA (Central Indiana Council on Aging), which serves elderly and disabled individuals in Indianapolis. At one meeting, it was announced that we had a waiting list of over three thousand seniors who needed help in some way. In fact, the number-one way to get off the list was to pass away! I knew that there must be some way that I could help these individuals.

At the same time, Dave Boyer was helping with several construction projects for needy individuals. He had recruited a team of men at St. Luke's that was willing to donate a Saturday here and there to help. Jayne Thorne, our staff member of Community Ministries, knew both of us and made the introduction. We brainstormed how we could develop a program to do construction projects for seniors and disabled folks.

Dave and I met with an individual at Second Presbyterian Church who was building ramps for seniors every weekend in the summer. They had developed a ramp design that could be built and installed in one day without using concrete (so it would not have to "set" for a few days). Some of their ramps were taking a month to build so they could only help four or five families in a summer. We knew we could improve on the process! We didn't know, however, where we could get the money to purchase supplies or how we would recruit volunteers.

The next month, St. Luke's was launching T.I.M.E. ministries, and fairs were scheduled to notify and recruit volunteers for various programs throughout the community. Dave and I printed information about our idea and stood at our booth hoping we could recruit a few volunteers—we had 49 people sign up!

The last hurdle was the money, which did not prove to be a hurdle at all. The CICOA board gave $30,000 toward our program if the ramps were built for CICOA clients. Second Presbyterian Church committed $5,000 per year, and St. Luke's provided some grant funding.

Now in our third year, we are building two ramps per week! We have a team that does the pre-cutting and assembly during the week and two other teams (made up of volunteers from both churches) that build the ramps on Saturdays.

What a great success and a blessing to help others in our community.

Oh God, we pray for all persons with conditions that cause them to be home-bound. May they feel your healing presence and loving support from the followers of Jesus, amen.

8
Cookies

By Dawn Bick

"Therefore let us stop passing judgment on one another. Instead make up your mind not to put any stumbling block or obstacle in your brother's way"
(Romans 14:13, NIV).

A service initiative was starting at church and I wanted to get involved. I didn't expect my husband to want to be involved. Although he is a loving and caring husband and father and was raised in a Catholic church, he had never expressed an interest in doing service projects at church. So, when this service initiative began, I fully expected to be volunteering alone.

That Sunday, we sat in church listening to the minister talking about the announcements and the new T.I.M.E. initiative, and she mentioned a specific opportunity to "get your T.I.M.E. minutes done." The opportunity to volunteer was decorating cookies for shut-ins. It sounded low-key, something I could bring the children to help with, and easy. It was exactly what I was looking for.

After we got home that afternoon, we discussed the announcements and what items we felt we might get involved with. I casually mentioned that I thought about doing the T.I.M.E. initiative with the cookie decorating and to my surprise, my husband was interested in it, too. Over our ten-year marriage, I have learned to take him up on his volunteer opportunities as soon as possible, because he may change his mind.

So, we arrived at church on the scheduled day to decorate cookies. We enjoyed meeting some new people and decorating cookies. As the time was winding down, the men started taking tables down and the women were cleaning up. It was announced that they needed volunteers to deliver knitted scarves and the decorated cookies to the shut-ins in the community; they had maps from church ready to go. Now, I don't remember that as being part of the initial deal and I thought for sure my husband would never go for that. Driving up to someone's home, whom we don't know, giving them a gift from the church, and possibly having to engage in conversation was way out of my husband's comfort zone.

I was so proud of the man I married as he walked over to the table, picked up three maps of homes that were on our way home and asked me to get cookies and scarves. The cookies and scarves were left on porches and in mailboxes, since none of our recipients were home, but I felt the experience was very rewarding. My husband took the initiative to bring others joy, and doing so brought me closer to him and to God. I was blessed as our family reached out to others in the community. Now my husband even volunteers in the nursery on Sunday mornings and wherever he is needed, assisting teachers, and just being willing and available to help. God reaches out to all in service: the person receiving the service, the person doing the service, and those witnessing the service.

Lord, take away my assumptions and lead me to help others through encouragement and love.

9
Working and Resting in the Love of God

By Betty Brandt

"And a second is like it: 'You shall love your neighbor as yourself.' On these two commandments hang all the law and the prophets" (Matthew 22:39-40).

Every time I walk into St. Luke's United Methodist Church's Spiritual Life Center, my eyes are drawn to two stained glass windows created by stained glass artist Minnietta Millard. They represent "Journey In" and "Journey Out," and are a constant reminder to me of the rhythm that defines my life.

Ever since I was a little girl, I have been drawn to a life of service. My mother and grandmother modeled this pattern and I followed their lead. Recently mission trips have been my service opportunity choice—Habitat for Humanity projects, a medical mission to Honduras, a Global Peace Initiative trip to Jamaica. Since 1995 I have traveled at least twice a year inside and outside the U.S. At first I was able to do manual labor. My favorite task was vinyl siding. Then about five years ago I was diagnosed with rheumatoid arthritis and thought my mission trip days had ended. Instead, I looked at what else I could do and found a role as a cook, as a wannabe optician, and as a planter of sunflower seeds. All of this is my "Journey Out."

During this same time period I became involved with the creation and development of a new ministry at St. Luke's—the Spiritual Life Center. This new ministry focuses on inward spirituality: meditation, yoga, contemplative worship, healing, visual arts, spiritual formation, and labyrinth walking. My own spiritual journey and the journey of the Spiritual Life Center became intertwined as I learned about and practiced all the programs I was helping to create. So finally I found a personal balance between my interest in the needs of the larger world and my pull towards the growth of an inner world—the "Journey In."

Corrine Ware, in her book *Discover Your Spiritual Type*, adapts the work of Urban T. Holmes to teach her readers about four approaches to the discovery of the Divine: Head, Heart, Mystic, and Kingdom. I have used her work to introduce lots of people to their own spiritual workings, and to help them better understand the spiritual diversity in our congregation and in our families.

Most of my mission trip buddies fall into the Kingdom category. They find God with a hammer in their hands as they build wheelchair ramps, frame new houses, and make roof repairs. Most of my Spiritual Life Center friends fall into the Mystic category and are drawn to times of silence, the works of Eckhart Tolle, icons, and the gifts of spiritual healing. I can see that in the future these two groups will more and more need to learn from each other.

My job is to form a bridge between these two loving groups of people. As their internal cups overflow, the Mystics will want a concrete way to serve all of God's creation and can be encouraged to take what they have developed on their inward journey out into the world where peace and calm are greatly needed. The Kingdom workers can relieve the stress created by the over-whelming needs of the world by journeying inward to find an entirely new understanding of the love of God awaiting them. Both groups will be blessed and strengthened by meeting and knowing the other.

Would you call yourself a Mystic or a Kingdom Maker? Do you have a symbol (like my stained glass windows) that can encourage and remind you of your personal journey in and out? Can you think of ways to develop the part of you that is not well known? You owe it to yourself to find people and ways to connect you to all your available experiences of the Divine. Find this balance in your service/spiritual life! Work and rest in the love of God!

Oh God, thank you for those who express their love for you through the inward journey of prayer, study, and meditation, and thank you for those who express their love for you and others through compassionate acts of service, amen.

10
The Right Thing to Do

By Donna Scheid

"He answered, 'You shall love the Lord your God with all your heart, and with all your soul, and with all your strength, and with all your mind; and your neighbor as yourself.' And he said to him, 'You have given the right answer; do this, and you will live.' But wanting to justify himself, he asked Jesus, 'And who is my neighbor?'" (Luke 10:27-29).

Last fall, we had new neighbors move in across the street. I was absorbed in our son's illness when they joined the neighborhood so I didn't get a chance to meet them. All I knew was they were an older couple and their children lived outside of Indiana. I waved when I saw them but other than that I never had the chance to introduce myself.

One day in February, I noticed a lot of activity at the house and wondered if everyone was OK. I learned the next day that Larry, the man of the house, had passed away suddenly after suffering a heart attack at home. Needless to say I was shocked. I had just seen him on Saturday working in the garage but once again, I hadn't taken the time to stop and say hello.

A few days later after all their company had left, I finally went over to introduce myself. I just wished I was doing it under different circumstances. As we talked I learned that she was undergoing radiation and chemo treatments for breast cancer and was struggling with her own health. As she was telling me everything I thought to myself, how will she take care of this big yard? She explained that Larry had purchased a new riding lawn mower last fall and had been anxious to use it. She wasn't sure how she would be able to maintain the yard, and she was confident that she would not be able to use the new mower.

At that moment I knew what had to be done. I would do the yard work for her with the help of my family! If there's one thing I can do, it's yard work. I love being outside and enjoying the wonderful world God has given us. Even when I'm on my hands and knees pulling weeds.

Things have worked out perfectly. My son cuts the grass, my husband keeps the shrubs under control, and I pull weeds, edge, and trim the grass. Her yard stays in tip-top shape and she doesn't have to lift a finger. All she has to worry about is getting her strength back and getting well.

You may wonder why our family is doing the extra work when she could hire a service to do the work instead. We do it because it's the right thing to do. Everyone needs help at some point in life. Jesus was the best teacher when it comes to helping others. He was there to calm the seas, feed the five thousand, heal the sick, and help the poor. He's here with us in everything we do and say and he's here for us when we go to him in prayer.

What can you do to help a neighbor? In this busy world we live in we all need help sometime. It really is the "right thing to do."

Oh God, thank you for our neighbors, those who live nearby and those who live faraway. May we follow your command to "love our neighbor as ourselves," amen.

11
Finding Grace

By Lori Crantford

For by grace you have been saved through faith, and this is not your own doing; it is the gift of God–not the result of works, so that no one may boast. For we are what he has made us, created in Christ Jesus for good works, which God prepared beforehand to be our way of life (Ephesians 2:8-10).

I was part of a team that traveled to Eldoret, Kenya to create a documentary about the work being done in the field of treating HIV/AIDS patients by the Indiana University in Indianapolis and Moi University in Eldoret. As you can imagine, immersing yourself in that type of setting is a shock to the system. You've traveled thousands of miles, left your family and friends far behind, and suddenly the folks you're with take on a motley look. Everything starts to look and feel overwhelming, and you wonder what in the world you were thinking.

And then, in the midst of experiencing disease and poverty that will not be denied, that soaks itself into your very pores against your will, you sense transformation. Because the very people who are impoverished beyond belief, the very people who are carrying a disease that robs them of their families, their friends, and their jobs, and which society tries very hard to rob them of their dignity as well—these people instill in you miraculous hope and amazing grace.

While we were in Eldoret, we maintained a blog site. This is an entry I made about amazing Grace:

"I have a new friend. Her name is Grace. I met Grace, or rather Grace found me, at the AIM (AIDS Initiated Movement) meeting last week. She turned around, smiled, moved her chair next to mine and the rest is history. Grace is 31 years old ("and I hope to live to be 60, and I know I will!") and HIV positive, which is how all 87 people at that meeting introduced themselves. "Hi, I'm [name] and I'm HIV positive." Grace is a widow with five children. She will tell you that she is "living positively" and she is working hard. She lives with her parents and children on a small farm. She runs a charcoal shop and is busy trying to learn all sorts of income-generating tasks: soap making, paper making, whatever it takes. In addition to caring for her own children, Grace takes in orphans, up to 13 at one point, 7 right now. "I want my children to mingle with them, to not fear being an orphan," she explains to me. Grace and I met again the next day and I gave her one of my Lance Armstrong "LIVE STRONG" bracelets; these bright yellow bands are popping up all over the hospital.

"Today a package arrived for me via one of our favorite new friends, Steve, the Welsh surf-bum turned passionate/compassionate farmer. It was from Grace. She sent me a knitted purse, a pair of AIDS ribbon earrings, a photo of her with her oldest son and one of the orphans, and this note (framed by the paper Robin taught them to make at FPI): Hi Lori: I hope you are doing so well by coping with our climate in Kenya. My dear Lori, kindly accept my gift however it is as I wonder whether you would love it, though it is my wish you admire it please. My dear, kindly remember me when you are in your country together with my children and orphans. I wish you safe journey and may God bless you. Bye bye, your friend Grace.

"We can all use a little more Grace in our lives. I celebrate in Grace finding me in Kenya."

God show us moments of grace and let us shine our lights as beacons of grace and hope in this world, amen.

12
Finding T.I.M.E

By Mimi Brodt

"Whoever sows sparingly will also reap sparingly, and whoever sows bountifully will also reap bountifully" (2 Corinthians 9:6, NIV).

"Each man should give what he has decided in his heart to give, not reluctantly or under compulsion, for God loves a cheerful giver" (2 Corinthians 9:7).

When Together in Ministry Everyday (T.I.M.E.) was first launched, I was a stay-at-home mom who ran a small business from our home. My oldest son was in second grade, and my youngest was in a Mother's Day Out program just one morning each week. As I listened to the pastor talk about the importance of giving, I quickly began listing all the excuses I had for not participating. I was already over-committed. I already struggled to effectively run my business with so little time when both boys were in school, and I certainly did not need to add any stress to my life. Maybe God wouldn't notice if I just kept my head down and tended to my work and family. Someday when I have more time to give, I will.

The idea of T.I.M.E. kept creeping back into my thoughts. A few Sundays later, I read in the bulletin that Meals on Wheels was seeking drivers to deliver meals. When I got home, I added "Call Meals on Wheels" to Monday's list of things to do.

I have been a Meals on Wheels driver now for several years, and it has been a perfect way for me to give at this point in my life. In fact, when I see "Drive for Meals on Wheels" on my list of things to do for the day, I find my heart filled with joy, even before I've driven the route. Just knowing that I'm going to spend a couple hours giving to others gives me a boost. And when my children go with me, I love seeing them learn and grow from the experience.

Once when the three of us delivered meals, our first stop was to an elderly woman who is a regular on the route. She clearly looks forward to her delivery each and every day. I honestly believe that she appreciates seeing someone at her door more than receiving the food.

Her eyes light up when I have my two boys with me. While we can't stay long because we have other hot meals to deliver, we always spend a few minutes talking with her. We tell her about that week's sporting events or piano recitals, and she always goes to her kitchen to see if she has a piece of candy, gum, or an apple for the boys. In fact, once when she didn't have anything, she opened the Meals on Wheels sack we had just given her and pulled out a package of cookies. She insisted they share the treat.

As we drove away that day, my oldest son asked why she gave away her food. I explained that he made her day a little more special, and she wanted to give him something in return. Then I thanked God for the opportunity to serve those in need, and for the wonderful lessons it has given my children.

Thanks be to God for his indescribable gift! Amen!

13
Frankencat

By Robin Howard

"Now there are varieties of gifts, but the same Spirit; and there are varieties of services, but the same Lord; and there are varieties of activities, but it is the same God who activates all of them in everyone" (1 Corinthians 12:4-6).

The year I turned twenty-one I learned some of the hardest lessons of my life, and one of my greatest teachers was a very ugly cat. I was working and going to school full-time and not enjoying either. I was completely at a loss for what to do with my life. I knew I wanted to do something that was joyful and contributed to the greater good, but I didn't know what that was. I'd just bought a duplex on the wrong side of a town where I didn't know anyone; the day I moved in, I sat on the floor and cried. The former owners had left piles of garbage, cockroaches, and seven cats.

I felt it was my civic duty to find good homes for the cats instead of just turning them out, so I put an ad in the paper. In the weeks it took me to clean, fumigate, and paint, I found homes for six of the cats. The seventh, though, was a problem. He wasn't exactly a kitten, plus he was the ugliest cat I'd ever seen. He looked like somebody had made him out of leftover parts. He was the color of rusted pipes and he had short legs that made him look like a parade float. I started to call him Frankencat. Prospective owners would come to meet him and promptly take off running.

After several weeks I was beginning to worry that I'd never find a home for him. Frank (for short), however, was not worried. When people came, he'd purr and be friendly and then when they'd leave he'd sit in the window and watch the birds. He never took a single rejection personally and he never seemed to doubt that his family was coming to get him.

One Sunday afternoon the phone interrupted my black mood and new prospective owners asked if they could meet the cat. So many people had passed on Frank that I didn't get my hopes up anymore. Soon a family pulled up and the husband and wife walked arm in arm up the steps. They sat in the porch swing and their little boy waited excitedly while I went to get Frank. The man took Frank from me and put him in his wife's lap. True to form Frank snuggled up and began to purr. The woman smiled and petted him. I watched in disbelief. No lame excuses, no horrified looks? What was she, blind?

"He's so soft!" she said. I think Frank smiled.

"My wife is blind," the man said, "and our son just started school. She wants a cat to sit in her lap and keep her company during the day."

"He looks like a marble!" the little boy said. "Dad, can we call him Marble?"

"Does he have a name?" the man asked. "Fr…" I started, and then I stopped myself. "No. He doesn't."

And so Frank not only got a family, he got a job—and one that he was good at! That cat taught me a very important lesson that day; not every opportunity will work out—but the *right* opportunity will work out. And until then, it's good to do stuff that makes you happy until the doorbell rings and it's time to go.

God, thank you for the gift of pets and the joy and comfort they give us, amen.

14
Get Out There!

By Tony Hunley

"'Let the little children come to me, and do not hinder them, for the kingdom of God belongs to such as these. I tell you the truth, anyone who will not receive the kingdom of God like a little child will never enter it.' And he took the children in his arms, put his hands on them and blessed them" (Mark 10:14*b*-16, *NIV*).

A couple of years ago, at the end of a six-month-long program sponsored by our Men's group, six men and I were challenged to do a service project for our community. To be perfectly honest, I wasn't too excited to rise to the challenge. I have always defined my ministry as building people up so they can go out and transform our world. I've often felt that Christians can get so involved in doing ministry in the community that they neglect to minister to themselves and each other. However, we are called by Jesus to do both of these, both are important and interrelated. It is an art to balance these two pieces, an art that had been out of balance for me. So, I decided to rise to the occasion and get out there in the community and do Christ's work.

After discussing many ideas, the guys and I decided we wanted to work with children. One of our emphases in Men's Ministry has been the importance of fathers and positive male role models in the lives of children. It's not that we belittle the impact that mothers have on children, but rather, we recognize the fact that many children are growing up without a father or positive male role model in their life. Some of that is due to men with unbalanced lives who are not giving their families priority. However, it is also attributed to families with physically absent fathers for a number of reasons.

We were emotionally torn up by the story of one particular elementary school in central Indianapolis. The statistics were staggering: only one in five children there had a dad in the home. Some had never known their dad, some lost them too early in their young lives, and still others had dads in jail. We had no lofty ideas that spending a day with them would make up for that loss in their lives, but we thought it could at least show them that there are men in this world who want to spend time with them.

We met a group of eight fourth- and fifth-graders at their school one spring morning and took them to a team ropes course. When we picked them up, they were polite, yet quiet as church mice. It was difficult to get them to tell us what kind of juice they wanted, let alone anything about themselves. We pushed on. We spent the day with them climbing ropes, playing "Poisonous Peanut Butter Pit" and other team development games, and flying down the zip line. By the end of the day, we didn't recognize the children. They were laughing, joking around, telling us about themselves, and genuinely having a great time.

I'll never know if those eight children will remember those church guys that took them to the ropes course, but my hope is they at least got a chance to realize there are compassionate men in this world who care what they have to say. My prayer is they find that in a more permanent sense. We were so amazed at what took place that day. It changed use forever.

My advice? Get out there! Get out of your comfort zone. Take some friends with you and see what God has in store for you! And, be sure to keep yourself spiritually refreshed.

Holy and loving God, teach us to be Christ-like in all our endeavors. Remind us that there are many children with many needs all over your world, needs that can be met when we heed your call. Help us to get out of our comfort zone and reach out in compassion to our neighbors. And, remind us to care for ourselves and each other so that we can continue your work, amen.

15
God's Plan

By Marion Miller

"'I know the plans I have for you'," announces the Lord. 'I want you to enjoy success. I do not plan to harm you. I will give you hope for years to come'"
(Jeremiah 29:11, *NIRV*).

A few months ago, we reached out to a couple in need of counseling who were not members of our church. They were going through a really tough situation in their marriage. As a matter of fact, their marriage vows were being challenged, and everything they had planned and worked for and built their dreams on came to a shattering halt. During several counseling sessions, I found that they each had many different emotions related to this life-changing situation that had occurred in their marriage: panic, fear, humiliation, disbelief, devastation, loss, sadness, injustice, and anger. The wife wanted to end the marriage, because she had been touched at the depths of her very being—she felt utter betrayal by someone she had implicitly trusted.

However, in this awful moment came blessings—many, many blessings! God provided time and a place for her to heal by surrounding her with a friend from our care ministry to nurture her emotional needs. God has brought her to a place of acceptance and contentment, if not yet forgiveness. Since that time, she has come to see each day as an opportunity to live in the light of Christ. This did not happen in one moment. It happens over time, little by little, opening her heart and trusting again. This time her hope and trust is rooted firmly in Christ. The couple is still together and now members of the body of Christ.

I believe that God has a plan for each of us. God sees possibilities and opportunities that we may not see. We cannot control or always know the future.

God's plan for us might not be the same as our own dreams, goals, and desires. However, when we can trust that God's plan is our plan, then our lives hold promises and opportunities for us to bless the family of God in unique ways. Place your trust in God, who shows us that all things are possible. God works through us, drawing us together with the kind of spiritual understanding that makes our dreams a reality.

Our loving God, you created us individually; we have been custom made. Help us to understand that change and growth are often the blessings of try-ing situations in our lives. Bless those who help to care and nurture us through times of unforeseen crisis and circumstances. Thank you for providing us with unique qualities and abilities that enable us to commit our lives to you. Help us to know that your plan is the best plan for our daily lives. In Jesus our Christ we pray, amen.

16
God's Will Breakfast

By Norm Stuart

"Jesus said to them, 'Come and have breakfast.' Now none of the disciples dared to ask him, 'Who are you?' because they knew it was the Lord"
(John 21:12).

"Norm"

"Yes, who is this?"

"This is the Lord!"

"Yeah, right! Who is it really?"

"This REALLY is the LORD!"

"Oh my, is it my time?"

"No. Norm, you are not listening to what I am saying to you."

"You mean about feeding the homeless and needy at Fletcher Place Community Center?"

"Yes, that is what I have been saying to you."

"OK, after two years I get it! I will start next year!"

"NO! I want you to attend Lenten breakfasts now, and I will tell you what to put on some brochures and what to say."

"OK, whatever you want, but where will the people to help me come from!"

"You don't understand Norm, they will be helping ME! I can arrange that very easily."

"Can I just start on Tuesdays?"

"Yes, but I want you to start very soon."

So started our mission to help the people of near-downtown Indianapolis with the Lenten Breakfast volunteers. Soon we would have every Tuesday and Thursday covered with food, people to prepare and serve breakfast for up to

49

190 people. Then the call was to finish the job by starting Friday breakfasts. This meant that people at the center could have hot meals five days a week. Instead of St. Luke's doing all the meals, we would soon have nine other churches helping our mission. I personally called on a couple of churches to explain what we were doing, but God called on all who are helping or who have helped serve. So far more than 100,000 breakfasts have been served.

Once, my friend Joe and I went to one of the first Thursday meals and found we were the only two there. Joe called the director and told her we would have to cancel the morning meal. We could not prepare, serve, and clean up for a crowd by ourselves! Oh me of little faith; when called to do this mission I was told that everything would be provided to do the mission! The director told us that she had told countless people and had a sign out front telling about the hot meal that would be provided that morning. We hesitantly went up the elevator to the kitchen, and started to cook. Suddenly there were four volunteers from St. Luke's who had not signed up but had read of our need in the Sunday bulletin. The next few minutes brought four students from the University of Indianapolis, who were there to volunteer as a school project. You might think this was a coincidence; we don't. Imagine the leap from all-out fear to faith—an understanding that this was a call from God and that we were being provided with all we needed. All of us who help prepare and serve the meals have a feeling of extreme joy. That is why we call this mission "God's Will Breakfast" And it is!

Listen to what God tells you, and then do it!

God, you are so faithful to us! When you call us to a task you also supply us with all we need to fulfill it. Thank you for your faithfulness. Amen.

17
Gracias

By Bev Gallagher

"I was sick and you took care of me" (Matthew 25:36b).

I faced the medical mission trip to Honduras with a mixture of excitement and trepidation. Knowing only about ten words of Spanish was a bit of a hindrance, not to mention that the extent of my medical experience came from the perspective of patient rather than physician. Then there was the fact that I'd be away from everything familiar, comfortable, and predictable for nearly two weeks in a third-world country.

Yet twenty-eight of us from several different churches set aside our "normal" lives for twelve days to travel to Honduras, ride hundreds of miles in an uncomfortable, ancient bus, spend time and energy packing and unpacking supplies, speak halting Spanish, eat fried plantains prepared over an open fire, use an outhouse, bandage cuts, examine rashes, paint little girls' fingernails, take blood pressure, clean out ears, fit eyeglasses, count and package pills, wipe tears and noses, and do dozens of other out-of-our-comfort-zone tasks.

And to what end? For most of us the answer lies in a quote from St. Teresa of Avila who lived during the sixteenth century. She said, "Christ has no body on earth but yours, no hands but yours, no feet but yours. Yours are the eyes through which Christ's compassion for the world is to look out; yours are the feet with which He is to go about doing good; and yours are the hands with which He is to bless us now."

In providing primary medical care to three thousand terribly disadvantaged native Honduran villagers, we had the privilege of being Christ's hands and feet, but we were the ones who were blessed. We were abundantly blessed by the smiles of gratitude, the touch of a hand, giggles from the children, the whispered "Gracias." At the end of our trip, we were reminded that each of us was leaving behind a piece of ourselves in Honduras. For me, it was a piece of my heart.

O God, thank you for your healing power and for using us to be channels of your love to persons in need, amen.

18
Have a Good Breakfast

By Robin Howard

"For this reason I remind you to rekindle the gift of God that is within you through the laying on of my hands" (2 Timothy 1:6).

I once read that the work God calls you to do is the place where your gladness and the world's deep hunger meet. Recently in a desperate search for gladness I told God "I'm just an artist, but whatever I have that you want, it's yours." Those are the magic words that landed me in Africa, cutting papyrus in a python-infested swamp.

By sheer coincidence I had met a man who was gathering a film crew to make a documentary about AIDS in Africa. By (divine) impulse I said "I want to go" and he put me on the team. I had no idea why I was going, but I knew I was meant to go. On the first few days of the trip I felt like the little sister who was tagging along with the big kids. I didn't know how to help with the camera equipment and I certainly couldn't offer any production advice. One day while the crew was meeting, I volunteered to go with Joe Mamlin, the field director for the AMPATH program, to pick up lunch.

As we waited for our food, Dr. Mamlin was talking about the complex problems of AIDS in Kenya. He said that they could give people medicine, but without income they would often go home and starve to death. He motioned to the landscape and said: "Look at all this papyrus. If we could get an artist here to teach them to make paper, they could make cards and export them. They could earn their own money."

"I'm an artist. I could teach them." I said in a squeaky little voice. And I spent the next few days scouring the markets for supplies, borrowing equipment, and cutting papyrus in the swamps. AMPATH had already established a small HIV-positive crafts co-op, and on the day of class nearly twenty-five HIV-positive men and women walked or hitched rides from their villages to learn papermaking. In broken Swahili and (what I'm sure were) funny hand motions, I taught them how to make paper from papyrus and trash. They learned fast, and soon paper was drying on every surface. At the end of the day the eldest had been elected to speak for all of the students. She said that they wanted to thank me for coming all the way from America to teach them, that they were honored to be my students and that they would work very hard to make good paper so I would be proud of them. I had no way to tell them that it was perhaps my greatest honor in life to have been their teacher and they had already made me as proud as I could ever be—both of their effort and to be "just" an artist.

Today, with the help of many people, the co-op has become a fair-trade certified Imani Workshop and they export some of the most beautiful handmade paper I've ever seen.

To anyone searching for gladness in their vocation, I would offer two pieces of advice: Whatever it is that you do, offer it up. Then have a good breakfast, because you're going to need your energy when God sends your assignment.

Thank you, God, for the gifts you have placed within us. Help us to use them in ways that bring glory to you and loving service to others. In Christ's name, amen.

19
Healing Ministry

By Sally Pearson

"When the sun went down, everyone who had anyone sick with some ailment or other brought them to him. One by one he placed his hands on them and healed them" (Luke 4:40, The Message).

I am blessed to participate in the St. Luke's Healing Ministry. Using a technique called the Pilgrimage Process developed by an Episcopal priest, we incorporate therapeutic touch, Reiki, and prayer to remove blocks to the body's natural process of healing. Clients are helped to relax on a massage table, while two healing partners perform the technique and pray to be channels for healing.

Our clients range from persons coping with psychological stress to those facing life-threatening diseases and accompanying treatments. Even though we don't ask for feedback, often clients relate remarkable results, ranging from a welcomed period of relaxation and refocusing, to relief of symptoms of side effects from chemotherapy, to full recovery from a Stage 4 cancer. Often our clients desire to learn the technique and become healers themselves.

Jesus told his disciples to go out and heal the sick and Jesus healed many people of all types of physical and mental illnesses by "laying his hands on each one." Physiological and medical scientists are amazed with new research that shows how our emotions and thoughts can actually change cellular structure. How can we rule out the power of touch and prayer? As I say frequently, "There's always more to the story." I am also blessed, along with the client, to feel the connection with the Spirit, the power of that flow of healing energy, and the human connection of being in service.

Living and Loving God, we know that it is through you that all healing takes place. Help me to be open to your healing powers and be a channel for your healing love. May I not hesitate to reach out to those in need to provide compassion, comfort, and hope, amen.

20
It's Never Just One Person

By Larry Welke

"All this is from God, who reconciled us to himself through Christ, and has given us the ministry of reconciliation" (2 Corinthians 5:18).

After we participated in Jayne Thorne's Race Relations classes, took her facilitators training, and participated in her Race Relations Committee, Jayne asked a group of us what we wanted to do with our new awareness of the race problem in our community.

That was a fair question deserving a fair response, and yet nothing really came to mind that seemed do-able. On the one hand, I had visions of several grand projects that would forever change the world, all of which had the common characteristic of being well beyond my ability to execute. But for the life of me, I couldn't see myself doing anything remotely practical or worthwhile.

After a few months of frustration at not being able to come up with my response, rather than reaching outward I began looking inward. What was I doing with my everyday life that might be an answer to Jayne's challenge? At the time, I was running a small multimedia company, doing video commercials for local businesses. It was an exercise, not necessarily a challenge.

As I thought about that business, its workforce and customers, I realized that there was a noticeable absence of African-American participation. Further investigation provided much of the reason for this: the public school system wasn't training inner-city youth in the necessary technology. Due to tight budgets and limited resources, a whole segment of our young people was being excluded from an exciting and growing employment opportunity.

I realized that I could probably organize a not-for-profit company that could fill that void; all I needed was a bit of support and a business plan. I got the support from Ball State University and IUPUI (Indiana University/ Purdue University Indianapolis)—and my friends at St. Luke's UMC. The universities gave me student interns to work with; friends at St. Luke's gave me the verbal and moral encouragement, and the financial backing to carry the project forward.

The not-for-profit we formed, Children Without Limits, Inc., had nine students from two schools in its first year of operation. In the second year, we had twenty-four students from four schools. And now, planning for our third, we'll have fifty students from ten schools. We've modified the curriculum each year as we better understand the needs of our students, what motivates them and how they learn. This coming year we'll add a Film Festival for the students to show off their work and accomplishments. Possibly within the year we'll also add another inner city because we believe our mission is portable, scalable, and valuable,

The students who participate come back for another year. Several who have graduated from high school have gone on to pursue university work in multimedia and film. The social good of our video storytelling project is beginning to show. It might have been my idea but I'm the first to point out that it was the support and involvement of a lot of our congregation that made it all happen.

We thank you, God, for persons who use their gifts and talents in ministries of reconciliation, amen.

21
Jesus on the Greyhound Bus

By Brian Durand

"Be wise in the way you talk to outsiders; make the most of every opportunity. Let your conversation be always full of grace, seasoned with salt, so that you may know how to answer everyone" (Colossians 4:5-6, *NIV*).

Sometimes we think church mission work is something we have to go out of our way to do for someone else. We need to serve someone else to be in mission. Ultimately, though, Christian mission isn't about serving someone because we have something and he or she doesn't. When we approach mission this way our ego stands in the way of Christ-centered relationships. Instead, the heart of mission is recognizing that God loves each and every one of us, and everyone deserves to know the transforming power of that love. I recently remembered this lesson on, of all places, a Greyhound bus.

Our youth mission team was traveling to New York City to feed and clothe the homeless, and Greyhound was the most economical and convenient option. Not many groups travel Greyhound, as we learned from their inability to fathom a group of our size on their buses. One reason groups don't travel this way is the grueling travel schedule; seventeen hours with stops every two hours, making sleep virtually impossible. Our large group also meant the bus was packed. About halfway into our trip, we stopped in Pittsburgh. We had to get off the bus as it was cleaned and refueled. We stood in line, tired and worn out, waiting to get back on the bus. The youth were asking if we could get on first since we were a group. What they really wanted was to get on first to save seats and avoid sitting next to someone on our bus who obviously hadn't bathed in some time and appeared homeless. I wanted the trip to be as smooth as possible so we would be ready for the mission work we were to do in the city, so while I confronted our collective desire for privilege, I also positioned the group to get on first.

As we re-boarded the bus and took our seats next to each other, I watched the homeless man step onto the bus and suddenly felt a wave of emotion. I was the leader of this trip, and yet I was so focused on future service work that I missed how Jesus leads us into mission. Jesus would have stepped on the bus and sat next to that homeless man. He would have engaged him in conversation and made sure that in the span of our bus travel together he knew that God loved him. While I wish I could say that I got up and sat next to the man on the trip, I didn't. Yet I did enter into our mission work in New York with a powerful reminder that we are called as Christians to share God's love in relationship with others, offering identity to those who are outcast, fellowship to those who are lonely, and hope to those who are lost. We don't have to go out seeking opportunities to serve to be in mission. The chance to share the love of God with someone is right in front of us most every day.

Loving God, help us to love as Jesus loved. Guide us into relationships where we can share the powerful love that we know in Christ, amen.

22
Keep It Going Around

By Karen Patton

"Do not judge, and you will not be judged; do not condemn, and you will not be condemned. Forgive, and you will be forgiven; give and it will be given to you... for the measure you give will be the measure you get back"

(Luke 6: 37-38).

I leaned my head down to paint behind another toilet in the boy's locker room. I wondered about my first mission trip, "Is this what 'giving' is all about?" Two days later I cleaned my paint brush and began sorting mountains of bags stuffed with donated clothes; children's here, men's there, toys over there. I asked myself again, "What are you doing here?"

At the end of the day I heard stories about the rough roads experienced by those we were helping. I began to connect my bathroom paint and the mounds of donated clothing with the actual human beings who needed so much.

After dinner we gathered in groups to play euchre and dominos. Exhausted, the final lights went out and the fun and silliness began. Surprise visits and tricks were played on those who had hoped for a restful sleep. The friend-ships, the laughter, the sharing; maybe this is what Jesus wanted for us.

On Saturday evening, we were invited to travel back into the hollers of the Kentucky hills for their once-a-month square dance. An hour of twisting turns to the right and quick cutbacks to the left through pitch-black woods on dirt roads left our stomachs as well as our minds wondering, "What does this have to do with helping folks that need so much?"

We pulled up to a one-room schoolhouse turned community center with lights and sounds of down-home country music. The door was open and a crowd of smiling faces greeted us with "thank you" and "glad to have you." The fiddles and banjos played lively tunes while ladies showed off their quilting projects and homemade jams. The caller slowed things down until we learned the do-si-dos and allemandes. We joined everyone with excitement as the famous cake walk began. We won two cakes! We fit in, we were accepted into their culture, and we were a living chapter of their lives. They, too, became a living chapter of my life.

As I tried to answer my own questions, I thought back on my life: the mistakes, the regrets, the need for forgiveness, and the need to start over. I am grateful that the Lord sent me help, that God forgave me and gave me opportunities to experience and grow. How truly blessed I am! Not through my own doing but from the hard work, sacrifice, and love given to me by the Lord and his angels—they will never know how they helped me.

I've always relied on the phrase "what goes around comes around" as an answer to many negative situations. But God did not bless me in a negative way. God has shown me that "What goes around, comes around" also applies to God's blessings. Sometimes I see them outright and others appear from faith and trust. So it was with my first mission trip.

Dear Jesus, let me follow your way and do for your people as you have done for me. As I have not seen all your blessings, I may not see the results of what I have done for others, but I do this work in your name, amen.

23
Lewis

By Sara Cobb

"His divine power has given us everything we need for life and godliness through our knowledge of him who called us by his own glory and goodness. . . .For this very reason, make every effort to add to your faith, goodness; and to goodness, knowledge; and to knowledge, self-control; and to self-control, perseverance; and to perseverance, godliness; and to godliness, brotherly kindness; and to brotherly kindness, love" (2 Peter 1: 3, 5-7, NIV).

"But the fruit of the Spirit is love, joy, peace, patience, kindness, goodness, faithfulness, gentleness and self-control. Against such things there is no law"
(Galatians 5: 22-23, NIV).

Lewis responded as you might expect from any eleven-year-old boy. "I know I need two more hours of community service for Boy Scouts, but I'd really like to stay home tonight." We were heading to Wheeler Mission to assist in serving meals to homeless men on a Sunday evening. Lewis was quiet in the car all the way downtown. I chatted about the important role Wheeler Mission plays in our community, recalling some information about Wheeler Mission from its website. When we arrived, Lewis was wide-eyed. For the first time, this suburban middle school student came face to face with homelessness. The men filed into the dining hall to get their food and drinks. Each and every one of them spoke to Lewis, thanking him for the food and for his time. Over the course of our two-hour shift, Lewis' wide-eyed look softened into one of empathy. He saw humans treating other humans respectfully, thoughtfully, and with gratitude despite the fact that they have little, if anything, to their name. In his eyes, I saw the question, "How can some of these men who have so little seem to have so much?" During our ride home, the questions flowed.

Thoughtful questions like, "Why are they homeless?" "How can they work their way out of being homeless? "How long can they stay at Wheeler Mission?" "After that, where do they go?"

On the way home, Lewis and I talked about the simple expressions of appreciation the men showed us. We expected to give of ourselves for two hours and return to the comfort of our suburban home comforted by the thought that we had done something good for others. But we came home with much more than we ever expected. We were inspired by a group of men who had nothing but still were appreciative of the small service we were able to provide. Much to our surprise, we were not the ones giving. The men who had so little were showing us brotherly love that exceeded anything we could have imagined. They gave us far more than we could have ever given them.

So be thoughtful, observant, and prayerful today about the people God brings into your life. How are they modeling Christian behavior and what can we do to more closely model that behavior ourselves?

God, give us hearts that are open to giving and receiving. Bless our ministry efforts and let us be a blessing, amen.

24
Losing a Child

By Marsha Hutchinson

"And he took them up in his arms, laid his hands on them, and blessed them"
(Mark 10:16).

The caller identification displayed the name of a friend with whom I had not talked in a long while. Anxious to reconnect and catch up, I quickly answered the ringing phone, but her voice sounded troubled. I soon learned this call would be much more than a time of friendly chatter.

My friend told me about a wonderful young couple whose four-month-old baby had recently died during a fairly routine surgical procedure. While these adoring parents held their son's blanket and pacifier, assured they would be returning home in a few hours, the medical team walked into the waiting room to deliver the life-changing message—their beloved son, their only child, was gone. There could be no worse nightmare for a parent.

My friend asked me to reach out to this family, especially to the young mother whose grief was understandably overwhelming. Remembering that I had started a support group for pregnancy losses and losses after birth, my friend cried out in desperation, "Is there anything you can do for them?"

How I wanted to answer her question with, "Sure, I can make the pain go away by telling her God loves her baby and his parents." Of course, this state-ment is true. God does love them, and God weeps with them, but for now those truths do not fill the empty arms of bereaved parents. What this grieving mommy and daddy needed were the arms, ears, heart, and tears of Christ that can be felt through those willing to walk into "the valley of the shadow." They needed a phone call that said, "I want to talk about your little boy"; they needed a hug that said, "I am so sorry for what you are going through"; and, they needed the reassurance, "I'm here for you whenever you need someone."

Days, weeks, months, and a year went by. Each week we cried, talked, remembered, and honored a little life lost too soon, and then we heard the news, "I'm pregnant!" The joy was over the moon, but the words that came next were those of a miracle when she said, "I would never have tried to have another baby if it hadn't been for your support, your love, and your care. Now I know what God is like."

This young couple can now be seen in the park, at the museum, or just walking along the street where they live, enjoying their adorable two-year-old second son, a gift from God.

Loving Lord, thank you for precious life and for your loving arms that reach out even in the darkest of days. Your steadfast love never fails as we walk this earthly journey with our friend, our Lord and Savior, Jesus Christ, in whose name we pray. Amen.

25
Michael

By Beth Fried

"Every time you cross my mind, I break out in exclamations of thanks to God. Each exclamation is a trigger to prayer. I find myself praying for you with a glad heart" (Philippians 1:3, The Message).

I met Michael in the pediatric ward of the Moi University Hospital in Eldoret, Kenya. He had been abandoned. He was small. His head was too big for his body. The staff estimated that he was about eight to ten months old, which made him certainly underdeveloped by our standards. He couldn't have weighed more than fifteen or twenty pounds. He was unable to sit up. He was obviously undernourished, but his HIV status was unknown (it is against the law to test without parental consent). He didn't cry. He made no baby sounds. I read once that babies in orphanages don't cry because it has never been reinforced to them that they will be attended to if they cry.

Michael had big eyes and seemed very curious. I don't know why, but Michael was mine as soon as I saw him. Every chance I got to go to the hospital I would visit Michael. I would sit and hold him and look into his eyes and talk to him. Just like my other babies, I can still feel him and smell him.

The hospital was able to find some of Michael's extended relatives and he lives with them now. He is with family. That is where he should be.

I am sure I will never see him again, but I think about him and pray for him every day. I often wonder if I affected his life in any way. Will it make any difference that once some Mzungu (white person) held him and talked to him?

Will it make any difference in his life that someone on the other side of the world is praying for him and loving him?

God, look upon Michael and his family and keep them safe and well. Make sure that he always knows that he is loved and he is valuable. Encourage his curiosity. Help him to become a sincere, intelligent, and compassionate leader. Let him and all children in need hear my prayers. Amen

26
Ministry Everyday

By Margaret Wood

"Then the King will say to those on his right, 'Come, you who are blessed by my Father; take your inheritance, the kingdom prepared for you since the creation of the world. For I was hungry and you gave me something to eat, I was thirsty and you gave me something to drink, I was a stranger and you invited me in, I needed clothes and you clothed me, I was sick and you looked after me, I was in prison and you came to visit me" (Matthew 25:34-36, NIV).

When I hear about people being "involved in ministry," I sometimes picture preachers or missionaries ministering or giving to others. It conjures up grand efforts and big gestures in foreign places…doing things and giving of self quite beyond my capacity. I can't be a minister or missionary. I have a family to care for and a full-time job to support that family! Sure, I (and my family) volunteer at church and other places in the community; but *minister*?

Then I remember Jesus' concept of ministry described throughout the New Testament. Jesus gave of himself to individuals in everyday situations and in everyday places. In fact, he really broke down ministry to these simple terms: "I tell you the truth, whatever you did for one of the least of these brothers of mine, you did for me" (Matthew 25:40, NIV).

There is opportunity to be in ministry everyday! Sometimes we just need to remind ourselves that every person we encounter presents an opportunity to share the love of Christ. It doesn't take an earthquake or tsunami to find people in need.

Many years ago while on a vacation in Jamaica, my husband and I were on a shuttle bus. The Jamaican driver was very friendly and we started up a conversation with him. He had clipped to his visor a picture of a young girl whom we soon found out to be his daughter. When he spoke of her you could see his love and devotion and his desire to care for her. As we talked more we realized that his family didn't have much money and he was doing anything he could to provide for them. That's when the "ah ha" hit us! Right there in that moment we were being confronted with a brother in need. Jesus' words came to mind (ironically, to both of us simultaneously); here was an opportunity, better yet a calling, to show the love of Christ. Our lives have been abundantly blessed—we are to be sharing that blessing! When we got off the bus, we slipped a heavy tip into our driver's hands. His eyes lit up and filled, and he thanked us profusely. As we walked away, our own hearts and eyes were filled with the joy of giving. And how easy it was to help another!

Dear Lord, please keep in our minds and in our hearts, in every moment, the idea that we can be ministers of your great love. Help us to see the needs of those in our everyday lives. Remind us to reach out with a smile, a hug, a prayer, or any other resource with which you have so generously blessed us. Amen.

27
Music Outreach — An Unanticipated Blessing

By Charles Manning

"Make a joyful noise to God, all the earth; sing the glory of his name; give to him glorious praise" (Psalm 66:1-2).

Joyful Sound is a small choir of around twenty singers which I direct. Instituted to provide musical leadership for the early-morning church service twice each month, this choir offers a less rigorous commitment for its volunteer singers than does the larger Chancel Choir of the church.

For several years the members of Joyful Sound have also committed themselves to taking their music beyond the church walls to seniors who live in various types of care-giving communities and to other civic organizations that provide a specialized environment for people with specific needs, such as children's hospitals, mission homes, hospital oncology units, and juvenile rehabilitation schools.

This music outreach effort has led the members of Joyful Sound rather unexpectedly into a powerful ministry that has become a source of joy, not only to our consistently appreciative audiences but also to the members of our choir. With the planning and leadership of one energetic and talented woman in the group, Joyful Sound has performed sacred music concerts, led hymn-sings, and presented soloists and small vocal ensembles in a variety of communities and institutions around central Indiana.

These events involve a fairly minimal amount of preparation for the choir, but always seem to immensely brighten and inspire the lives of those in attendance. The audiences are thrilled by whatever presentations we have to offer, and truly enjoy the interactive involvement in group singing and making song requests.

The unanticipated reward has come in the closeness and caring that has developed among the members of Joyful Sound. As they experience fellowship with the audience at a reception or meal after singing, they get to know each other better and experience the energy and vitality of Christian love. Each Christmas, Joyful Sound goes caroling at the oncology unit of St. Vincent's Hospital before gathering for our annual holiday dinner party. The joy of seeing the faces of the patients as they listen to the familiar Christmas songs, and often sing along with us, is something we look forward to with anticipation for weeks as we rehearse.

We pray that the music outreach efforts of Joyful Sound have provided some measure of spiritual aid to the audiences for whom we sing. But just as significantly, the experiences of giving the gift of music to the community have drawn our group much closer together as friends, Christians, and ministers of the gospel.

God, thank you for the gift of music and musicians. Thank you for the joy that comes from you to us through music. Amen.

28
My New Friend Russ

By Jim Thorne

"Love is patient; love is kind; love is not envious or boastful or arrogant or rude. It does not insist on its own way; it is not irritable or resentful; it does not rejoice in wrongdoing, but rejoices in the truth. It bears all things, believes all things, hopes all things, endures all things. Love never ends . . . And now faith, hope, and love abide, these three; and the greatest of these is love"
(1 Corinthians 13:4-8a, 13).

Russ was a quiet man who regularly attended the Men's monthly breakfast. I didn't know him well but was always glad to see him here visiting with other men and enjoying the program.

One day I learned that Russ was very ill and in intensive care at a local hospital. Hearing this news triggered a memory about our church choir. The Minister of Music had shared with me that his ministry went beyond music to include ministering to members of the choir and that the choir views itself as ministers to one another in times of need.

It occurred to me that the Men's breakfast could be more than a breakfast ministry. So, off to the hospital I went to visit Russ. On the first visit he was too ill to talk with me. I met his wife and some of the medical team. Interestingly, another Men's group member was on Russ' care team. Following my visit I spoke with the church Director of Care Ministry who personally visited Russ and his wife the following morning and arranged for a Stephen Minister to connect with them.

On subsequent visits I learned a lot about Russ and we became friends. He was quiet in manner but deep in substance. He was a loving husband and father. He had a strong faith. He had a good sense of who he was and a good sense of humor. He enjoyed reading and was glad when I loaned him some of my favorite books. We prayed together. We sat together. We talked. We enjoyed each other's company. A teenager in the church youth group also agreed to visit Russ in the hospital.

Russ' diagnosis was serious, but he regained strength and began to look forward to going home. Then his illness intensified and, taking a turn for the worse, he passed from this life into the hereafter. The Stephen Minister continued to support his wife. The teenager visited his wife. Men from the church mowed the lawn until other arrangements could be made.

The journey began with a quiet man attending and enjoying the UMM breakfast. The journey continued through the cycle of life, the making of friendships, the support of a church community, and a lesson that we are all here to be in mission to one another.

So, whatever your connections with individuals and groups, you are invited to think of what you are doing as part of a mission to be there for one another. And don't wait until illness strikes to really get to know the great guy or gal who seems a bit shy or quiet.

Oh God, thank you for your love that binds us together in this human family, and for those who share that love with all persons in need. Amen.

29
Oasis of Faith

By Sharon Holyoak

"Rejoice always, pray without ceasing, give thanks in all circumstances; for this is the will of God in Christ Jesus for you" (1 Thessalonians 5:16-18).

When the doors first opened to the church bookstore & gift shop, the truly inspired individuals who conceived the idea knew that they were inviting people into a beautiful environment that would provide a service to its members and create proceeds that could go back into various missions within the church. They could sell books for classes, Bibles, Christian literature, cards, and inspirational gifts in a quiet library setting. What it has become, in no small way to me, however, is one of the greatest blessings of my life and a far greater personal mission: to truly live in God's presence, to seek and share knowledge, and see each moment spent in this space as an invitation to connect with each individual who walks through its doors and share the love of Christ.

In the beginning, I didn't know how much strength I would gain on my own spiritual path or what a sacred place this would become for me, especially during difficult times in my life. I've been given a great gift and joy is contagious. There is an instant comfort level when people wander in. After all, it is a shop with gifts, jewelry, and great books; what's not to like? No one will preach to you or pressure you, but very often, although people will leave with a purchase, they are really here to share their story, to find peace and understanding. The Holy Spirit is very present in this place and there are many opportunities to listen, to be a witness to someone's pain or their joy. There will be a man who wanders in asking for a book on the afterlife, but much later reveals that his son is dying of cancer and he is trying to find answers.

Or a woman who is anxious to tell you that the clinging cross she bought for her friend was what got her through a difficult surgery. Sometimes it's a church member who lost her job and needs resources, support, or someone to pray for her. We share in the joys as well and hear how we are touching lives, lifting spirits, providing comfort to our church, community, and in our own small way, the world.

We search for and buy from companies around the world that are mission-based and support fair trade—companies that are trying to restore humanity, dignity, compassion, vitality and self-reliance to those most vulnerable on our planet. Our members are so willing to embrace diversity and the beautiful art that each culture brings. One example is a company that sells handbags made from recycled Mayan blouses. A Mayan woman can spend four to twelve weeks weaving up to eight hours a day to make one blouse. She weaves and embroiders designs that reflect her history and ethnic identity and becomes financially self-sufficient. Mother Teresa says, "Do small things with great love." For a little shop at the church, I guess that explains it best.

Oh God, thank you for the opportunity of loving and serving all the people we encounter today. Amen.

30
One Child at a Time

By Jayne Moynahan Thorne

"'Whoever welcomes this child in my name welcomes me, and whoever welcomes me welcomes the one who sent me; for the least among all of you is the greatest'"(Luke 9:48).

The T.I.M.E. initiative reminds us that we come to church to be transformed by God so that we might go out and transform the world into a compassionate, just, inclusive, and Christ-like community. This transformation can occur from hearing a sermon, a prayer, a conversation or a holy moment of any kind. In my case, it came from a new learning in a dialogue experience.

A few years ago I participated in a race relations study circle where my eyes were opened to a new concept—white privilege. I had unknowingly experienced this privilege, but suddenly I could see it all around me. Now that I had this knowledge, what would I do about it? In the race relations study circle, we had discussed education as the great leveler. Suddenly I had an "aha" moment. I can help in this area to level the playing field! My husband, Jim, and I chose to become a "Big Couple" through the Big Brothers, Big Sisters program for a ten-year-old African-American boy who needed support, guidance, and friendship to reach his potential. Our "Little Brother" was an at-risk child—single parent, no father in the picture, in poverty, not doing well in school, an older brother who was incarcerated and had become a father at sixteen.

We formed a friendship with our "Little" and worked with him to develop trust based on our commitment to him. We tutored him during his fourth-grade year to help him overcome two years of retention in his public school and he was promoted to fifth grade. We coached him to develop his leadership skills. We found out about a free school, the KIPP academy, a college preparatory middle school for at-risk kids, and helped him get in. He is now thriving and has set a goal of going to college and becoming a medical professional. Thanks be to God!

Have we transformed the world? Of course not! But we have helped one child to see that he is smart, capable and self-reliant, that he has support from two people who really care about him, that he can dream bigger and that there is a better way to live his life. In turn, our prayer is that our "Little" will lead the way for others in his family, his community and his world. All with a little nudge from T.I.M.E. reminding us that we are all together in ministry every day.

Oh God, thank you for teachers, mentors and positive role models for children everywhere. Amen.

31
People Who Need People

By Donna Scheid

"But a Samaritan while traveling came near him; and when he saw him, he was moved with compassion. He went to him and bandaged his wounds, having poured oil and wine on them. Then he put him on his own animal, brought him to an inn, and took care of him" (Luke 10:33-34).

I love musicals. Have you ever noticed how the lyrics to the songs can really hit home? Take, for example, the chorus from *Funny Girl*, "People, who need people, are the luckiest people in the world." Those words are so true. We all need people, and how lucky are we when people are there for us. That was the case when my son was diagnosed with non-Hodgkin's lymphoma.

My parents taught me the importance of helping others. They were always helping someone when I was growing up. It didn't matter who it was. If someone needed help they were there. And it didn't matter what help they needed. It could have been as simple as a meal for someone at church or cutting the neighbor's grass. Or it could have been the extreme of hanging wallpaper for someone or fixing their family car. My parents were always there to help. I took their example to heart and have tried to follow in their footsteps by helping people when they need it.

When my son was diagnosed with cancer, people were there to help. The problem was I had a hard time accepting their help. I don't think I knew how. I had always been on the giving end and not the receiving end, so I struggled to tell them what I needed when they asked. I felt guilty bothering them with my needs. So I would tell them politely that I didn't need anything when they asked.

Six years later my son's cancer returned. Those same people, along with many more, were there once again asking me what I needed or what they could do to help. This time I accepted their help with open arms and an open heart. I had learned that they needed me just as much as I needed them. I was the luckiest person in the world to have so many people who wanted to be there for me and my family.

In Luke's Gospel Jesus uses the parable of the Good Samaritan to explain how much people need people. What would have happened if the Samaritan hadn't seen the need of the beaten man and passed him by as he walked down the road?

That's what it's all about, "people needing people." Being there when the food pantries are empty or the snow needs to be cleared from the neighbor's sidewalk. Being there when your child's teacher needs an extra set of hands in the classroom. Being there to take a shut-in to church on Sunday morning. Being there when a friend's son is diagnosed with cancer and she's carrying the weight of the world on her shoulders. It doesn't matter what the need is, we just need to be there for each other just like our Heavenly Father is there for us.

Lord, thank you for being there for us. Help us to be there for others. Amen.

32
The Power of Prayer

By Larry Welke

"He was praying in a certain place, and after he had finished, one of his disciples said to him, 'Lord, teach us to pray . . .'" (Luke 11:1).

May 13 was simply another work day. The seminar I was hosting could have been better; at the end of the session I thought I could have done a better job of organizing it. The following day I went out for my usual morning run around the lake to further think about the seminar. I took note of the fact that one of the women in the neighborhood seemed to be walking faster than I was running. Ego rather than the more obvious physical anomaly caused me to call our family doctor when I returned home.

By the afternoon I was resting not too comfortably in the cancer ward of St. Vincent's Hospital. After seventy-six years of never missing a day of school or work I was diagnosed as having cancer of the lymph system, not the most common form of cancer, with only a 30 percent rate of survival. So started my new experience as an impatient patient, asking the usual and ridiculous question: Why me, God?

It became a learning experience in a way I never expected. Almost from day one, my fellow parishioners visited me with flowers, books, cards, and prayers. I had always categorized myself as a God-fearing, praying Christian but the emphasis was never on fearing and only nominally on prayer. I preferred to think of God as loving, not someone to be feared. And prayer was an interesting concept, but unproven in my lifetime.

Together in Ministry Everyday: 52 Devotions

As summer wore on, I heard of several groups praying for my recovery, and every one who came to visit my hospital room said a prayer before they left. I should mention that the first few weeks were rather touch and go. More than once, my hematologist left my room after his morning examination shaking his head—and I didn't have the courage to ask him why.

Then the medical reports began coming back with positive results. Several side effects were going away. Soon enough I was off the heart monitor, no more oxygen tubes, daily pill count reduced from twelve to three. And I wondered if there could be some kind of connection to all that prayer.

As I now look back on that hospital and rehab experience, I know that I owe my recovery, indeed, my survival, to those people who prayed for me. Many I knew, many I did not. I still don't know much about fearing God, but prayer has become part of my day and part of my life.

We thank you, God, for the healing power of prayer. Amen.

33
Pro Bono

By Kendall Millard

"What good is it, my brothers and sisters, if you say you have faith but do not have works? Can faith save you? If a brother or sister is naked and lacks daily food, and one of you says to them, 'Go in peace; keep warm and eat your fill,' and yet you do not supply their bodily needs, what is the good of that? So faith by itself, if it has no works, is dead" (James 2:14-17).

Several years ago, as a new lawyer in a Washington, D.C. law firm, I was asked if I would represent pro bono a Kenyan man who had been severely injured in the 1998 terrorist bombing in Nairobi. He had been working for the U.S. Embassy when the bomb leveled his side of the building. He woke up months later at the Walter Reed medical facility in Washington, D.C., blind, with shrapnel scars all over his face and body. The U.S. government had done an outstanding job helping his body heal, but was making plans to send him back home without any support on the Kenyan side. The man thanked God for the continued gift of life and the U.S. government for helping providing him medical attention after such a tragedy, but he felt helpless and hopeless at the prospect of returning to a country where, now blind and impaired, he would have no way of supporting his wife and four children.

I took the matter, not knowing anything about the relevant law or whether I could be of any use. After over a year of exploring options, however, the State Department agreed to offer him a job at the new embassy in Kenya, train him on a voice-activated computer to do his work, and provide some transition funds to get his family started again in Nairobi. Then the week before he was scheduled to return, the State Department unexpectedly asked me to return to Kenya with him, at its expense, to help him with his transition. Although I had never been to Kenya, we somehow figured out how to buy a house in a secure neighborhood, find a car for his wife to drive, and meet with his supervisors to work out the details of his employment at the embassy.

This client and his family have become dear friends of our family. We stay in touch by e-mail and have had the opportunity to see each other several times since then. I have returned to Kenya twice, both times loading up a suitcase of gifts that are difficult or impossible to obtain in Kenya, and despite my protests, they showed up to see me off at the airport with the suitcase full of Kenyan souvenirs for my family and friends.

This experience has become a cornerstone of my faith story. I took the case without knowing whether my newly minted law degree could be put to any good use in the world and ended up not only helping a family at a crossroads in their lives, but building friendships that will last a lifetime. I also fell in love with Kenya, and my time there inspired me to return with Rotary to support the Indiana University/Moi University HIV/AIDS project in Eldoret, Kenya.

Oh God, thank you for the opportunity to use our particular gifts to provide the loving service needed by those around us. Amen.

34
Singing a Song of Hope

By Mark Squire

"Are any among you suffering? They should pray. Are any cheerful? They should sing songs of praise" (James 5:13).

I suppose it started out with a pair of innocent enough questions: "So what do you really need?" and "How can we help?" Meeting with a missionary on furlough, we had heard stories of recent tragedy and continuing challenge in little, war-scourged Croatia. Ethnic hatred, bombed-out churches, shattered families. "What do you really need?" translated in our American minds to "What kind of fundraising can we undertake?" and "What kinds of materials can we acquire to send back with you?" We were ready to be bold with our safe generosity, ready to do what we were really good at.

Instead, we were asked to provide music. No, not recorded music, CDs to sing along with, or songbooks translated into a native tongue to sing from. No, the wily missionary was asking for human voices, singing in harmony. "Ever since the war, at Christmastime there has been an unnerving silence," we were told. "There are no Christmas songs being sung. The pain has been too great."

Christmas songs? During the busiest, most demanding season of the church music year? Traveling halfway across the globe? What about our church's famed Christmas concerts and beloved Christmas Eve services? And what about the singers' family lives? What about being away from friends and families during the holiday season? One soprano gulped, realizing that her first grandchild might be born while she was away. Would we be safe?

"There are no Christmas songs being sung. The pain has been too great."

Twelve singers and an associate pastor began to dream. We would depart shortly after the scheduled church concerts, rich with colored lights and orchestra and joyful carols. We would travel to a land of gray cold, of buildings riddled with bullet holes, toppled steeples, smashed villages, and areas still dangerous with landmines. We would be shuttled to and from small country churches, each bearing the scars of catastrophe. Bundled grandmas and a few small children were at some. The rest, we were told, had fled, and many had gone missing. We would sing in historic, unheated sanctuaries, some standing since the Reformation, with our breath fogging up our glasses.

We were met with tears, smiles, and then more tears. Warm, extravagant hospitality, even with limited means, contrasted the surrounding horror. Word was received, the soprano was now a grandma, and her joy overflowed, and was then translated, and a social hall or chapel would erupt with applause and smiles.

"Silent Night, Holy Night" gathered stranger to stranger, child of God to child of God, and as English words were followed by Croatian translation in obvious Midwestern American dialect, frail voices joined: *"...all is calm, all is bright...with the angels let us sing..."*

The singers received rapturous applause in a gilded university setting and were also featured on state radio broadcast, but it was in amidst the broken and despairing that God's richest grace and beauty seemed most realized. Transformation? It would be difficult to know where the greatest life-change was experienced. Many people heard and received the song of hope, but there are twelve singers and an associate pastor who continue to say their lives will never be the same again.

Oh God, thank you for the healing power of music. Amen.

35
Stephen Ministry

By Lisa Peters

"Whoever sows sparingly will reap sparingly. Whoever sows generously will reap generously...each man should give what he has decided in his heart to give" (2 Corinthians 9:6-7, NIV).

Several years ago my family was faced with dealing with my Dad's lung cancer. During his struggle we were made aware of Stephen Ministry. We were advised we could each be assigned a caregiver as we dealt with this situation. After my family's wonderful experience with the Stephen Ministry program I decided to take the course and become a Stephen Minister.

I met an incredibly loving group of people who helped nurture me through the outreach program. Little did I realize that not only did I use this training as a Stephen caregiver myself, but I tend to use it in my everyday work life as a supervisor to over fifteen women. All of these women come from different walks of life and vary in age from thirty-five to seventy-five. One is in remission from cancer, another is dealing with the recovery from her husband's second heart attack. We've been through divorces and births of grandchildren, through empty nesters watching their college-age children venture out on their own. Some struggle to balance schedules of school-age children and others pay babysitters just to work part-time.

Who knew so many years ago that my commitment to become a Christian listener would allow me to reach beyond the boundaries of my local congregation and nurture women all over central Indiana?

I remember a poem from my childhood, written by a classmate. He wrote,

"The world full of problems and mine so small, but in my mind they stand so tall." That's how it is for all of us. As we face life's trials they can seem "so tall!" I believe the knowledge from Stephen Ministry helped me become a good listener, pray according to what people truly needed, and share God's love to help them overcome whatever their trials were.

I began a program years ago to receive encouragement for the difficult problem that seemed "so tall" in my daily life. I ended my Stephen's experience with giving from my heart, truly listening, and sharing that God's love is able to carry all of us through.

Loving God, please bless us this day as we serve you and care for others. Amen

36
The Barbie Shoes: A Christmas Story

By Jennifer Todd

"On entering the house, they saw the child with Mary his mother; and they knelt down and paid him homage. Then, opening their treasure chests, they offered him gifts of gold, frankincense, and myrrh" (Matthew 2:11).

It was a hectic Christmas that year. In addition to the normal stress of shopping for two small children and extended family, holiday baking and cleaning, and decorating the house for company, I had agreed to coordinate the Christmas collections for our group of mothers of young children. Our group had "adopted" a needy family within our church: the parents were hearing-impaired, the father was Hispanic and spoke broken English, and they had a lot of children. Each child needed a basic set of clothes—underwear, socks, an outfit, a coat and a toy—all new items. In addition, the family wondered if we might have any hand-me-down clothes or toys for their children. Well, ask any group of mothers of young children if they have any hand-me-down items for a family in need and your prayers will be answered! I had more items than you could imagine.

I turned my attention to the collection of new items for the children. I made my list, I checked it twice, and I was short one pair of shoes for a five-year-old girl. It was too late to ask for help; I added it to my lengthy to-do list. For some reason that year every five-year-old girl must have needed a pair of tennis shoes because there were none to be found. I was stressed and frustrated as I visited store after store to find the right size. Maybe, I thought, I should just forget about it. After all, we had so many things to give the family, what difference would one pair of shoes make?

The final day before our collection was to be delivered, I had a small window of time before pre-school pick up. It was my final chance to find those shoes. The store had one pair of shoes in the right size—pink and purple Barbie shoes. I understood the risk—little girls either love pink and purple or they snub their noses in the air. Should I, or shouldn't I? I so wished I'd been able to find something more neutral. I carried those shoes around the store for fifteen minutes. I put them back, I picked them back up. And finally, I decided, they would have to do. At home that night, I kept looking at that box, still uncertain about my decision.

The next day, the shoes found their place with bags and boxes of other items for our family, an overwhelming assortment of items. I moved on to a wonderful family Christmas celebration, the shoe decision quickly erased from memory until sometime after Christmas, I received a note. It was a thank-you note from the father of our family, written in broken English. It said, "Thank you so much for all the things for my family, but, especially, my daughter, she loves the Barbie shoes." What difference would one pair of shoes make, indeed? A big difference! A happy, joyous Christmas for one little five-year-old girl.

I cried to think I almost gave up. I was filled with joy to know that treating that little girl as if she was my own and worrying and wondering if that pair of shoes would be "just right" was such a gift for me! We don't always get that gift, but it should never, ever keep us from giving!

O God, thank you for the gift of love you gave us in Jesus Christ. And thank you for the opportunity of sharing that love with others. Amen.

37
The Largest Family Ever

By Rev. Dr. Marion Miller

"Work hard to feed hungry people. Satisfy the needs of those who are crushed. The blessing will light up your darkness. And the night of your suffering will become as bright as the noonday sun" (Isaiah 58:10, NIRV).

For a three-month period as part of our T.I.M.E. *90 in 90* initiative, our church focused on reaching out to the community to those in need in the inner city. We wanted to feed the hungry and satisfy the needs of those who have been crushed and pushed to the margins of our society. Our intent was to be a blessing of hope and light into someone's darkness.

There was a man who stayed behind one of our evening worship gatherings for coffee and donuts. He was quite friendly and very talkative. He spoke with distinction in his voice, and it was very deep and strong. As I politely introduced myself, he thanked me for how warm and welcome we had made him feel. Then the distinguished gentleman began to share his story with me about his life.

The man said that he had suffered a terrible side of alcohol addiction in his past. He mentioned that he had been kicked out of his house, his mother's house, his brother's house, and his sister's house. Then with tears in his eyes he said, "There came a time there was no house to be kicked out of, so I was on the streets." I felt his pain as he shared his story. It felt like I could reach out and touch his suffering from his wounds.

But then he said, "I met a stranger, named Jesus, who rescued me! I am now a part of a recovery program." He continued, "I am thankful that Jesus, the stranger, did not give up on me. I now have a job, and the job gave me a home. And now that I have a home, the home game me a family. I am now a part of the largest family ever, the body of Christ."

We as Christians are God's arms, feet, and legs to help those who are in need. We are to feed hungry people, give them a place to stay, visit the sick and those who are in prison. We should not ask questions, or try to judge a person's situation, we should try to understand, and just do it!

Our loving God, we thank you for providing help and strength for us through others. You have a way of feeding hungry people, giving them a place to stay, and helping bring them out of darkness and into your marvelous light. Help us to know that you are always interceding on our behalf day by day. In Jesus the Christ, we pray. Amen.

38
The Shirt Off Your Back

By Chris Thornsberry

"I was naked and you gave me clothing . . ." (Matthew 25:36*a*).

A number of years ago I was at Inner Harbor in Baltimore, Maryland. It was a day for our mission team to just take a break and relax. We were in the Baltimore area working with a small group of people helping them with their new church start. Our objective was to work within the community providing Vacation Bible School opportunities.

Needless to say, I didn't feel as if I had been contributing much since this was not an area of ministry I was well versed in. I kept praying all week for the Lord to give me a chance to share his love with someone. My opportunity finally came.

I remember Inner Harbor that day. The tall ships were in town and it was a magnificent sight to be seen. I remember it was very hot and humid. I kept hoping that the sun would go behind the clouds and contain the swelter of the sun. No such luck though.

As we were finishing up lunch, everyone on the mission team discussed the week so far and all the opportunities they had of sharing God's love. My turn came around and I really didn't have much to say. I was embarrassed to say the least. We had already been there four days and I just felt like I had achieved nothing.

We walked out of the restaurant and I was feeling pretty full from the meal and pretty hot from the sun. I looked over to a resting area and saw a shirtless man.

He wore pants, but no shoes. Trying to escape the suns rays he had a piece of cardboard over his body. I slowly walked in his direction. I watched as people passed by him, laughing and calling him names. There were no bowls for money. No backpack with all his stuff. It was just him and the cardboard.

I asked God what I should do. At that point I knew what I had to do, but I honestly did not want to. I knew I had to give him my shirt. Now, being a bigger guy the last thing I wanted to do was take my shirt off in front of not only my group, but hundreds of strangers. However, I found the strength to give him my shirt. I removed the piece of cardboard from the man and helped him sit up. I then put my undershirt and t-shirt on him. His upper body was so red from the sun that I could tell even the slightest movement hurt. I told him that God was with him and would never leave him no matter what. I then prayed with him and went on my way wearing no shirt. I had to overcome my fear of how I looked in order to help this man. At the time I probably prayed something like this,

Dear God, I am so ready to show your love to someone. I am willing to do whatever it takes no matter what. Show me, O Lord, what your desire for me is today. I freely give myself and everything I have to you to be used. It is yours. Amen.

39
Thomas

By David Mitchell

"The LORD is my shepherd, I shall not be in want. He makes me lie down in green pastures, he leads me beside quiet waters, he restores my soul. He guides me in paths of righteousness for his name's sake. Even though I walk through the valley of the shadow of death, I will fear no evil, for you are with me; your rod and your staff, they comfort me. You prepare a table before me in the presence of my enemies. You anoint my head with oil; my cup overflows. Surely goodness and love will follow me all the days of my life, and I will dwell in the house of the LORD forever" (Psalm 23, NIV).

Being a Stephen Minister, I had the honor of having Thomas as my care receiver. He was forty-one years old, had multiple sclerosis, and had been told that he wouldn't live to see age eighteen. He was suicidal and had given up on life. As I got to know Thomas, I asked if he knew God. The answer was no. Through time, he did come to know God, learn how to pray, and discover how to read the Bible. He had a temper that he wasn't afraid to show. After becoming violent with me one evening, I said I was going leave, but not before we prayed. A few days later it happened again, but this time I wasn't going to pray. As I was walking out the door, he yelled, "But aren't you going to pray?" I said no, but that he could. He didn't know how, so I showed him. Then I left.

A few weeks later, he had a punctured lung. Within forty-eight hours, God called him home. Before his funeral service, his mother asked me to give the eulogy. She felt I knew Thomas more than anyone else. As God spoke through me, I realized how Thomas affected me. One of his favorite books of the Bible was the book of Psalms. He would read to me so many times. He especially loved Psalm 23. By the time of his death, he had memorized this chapter. So many times as a Stephen Minister, we don't think we accomplish much, but God uses us so much. I really didn't know how I could help Thomas, but now I see how God worked in both of us. God was with me through all this. I could have walked out when attacked, but God said to me that it wasn't time. Now I know why. He wanted me to be with Thomas. God has blessed me in many ways, and Thomas is one of them.

Oh God, thank you for your patience with us. May we be patient and loving toward others. Amen.

40
Toward the Light

By Chad Bocock

"You are the light of the world. A city built on a hill cannot be hidden. No one after lighting a lamp puts it under the bushel basket, but on the lampstand, and it gives light to all in the house. In the same way, let your light shine before others, so that they may see your good works and give glory to your Father in heaven" (Matthew 5:14-16).

In addition to trying to live every moment of my life in a way that is pleasing to God, I continually pray that he will help me be a light in the world. My hope is that the things I do will be seen as shining examples that point others to the love of Jesus Christ. I help with ushering at my church, which I believe assists both our members and our guests. I organize weekly meetings in my office for Bible study and discussions, which I believe helps others realize that we are taking the time out of our busy schedules to focus on God. Since I have had a brain injury, I assist the current patients at Hook Rehabilitation Services. I regularly take part in family education and speak with current patients and their families in order to help them understand that it's possible to rebuild their lives. I am one of the founding members of "Giving Sum," a new philanthropic organization in Indianapolis where we are directing funds that we have pooled together (starting with about $50,000 of our own funds). We then research the charities that we will ultimately help.

I have realized that becoming more involved has helped me to understand how gratifying giving really is. I know that I am truly blessed and hope that others can be blessed as well. I had always felt that I've had a good life. I just didn't previously have God at the center of it. I am eternally grateful that God has given me guidance to help me reprioritize my life. Now that God is the center of it, nothing can shake my faith. I've learned that it's a great way to live this life! I believe and rely on Romans 8:28: And we know that in all things God works for the good of those who love him, who have been called according to his purpose. I pray that God fills our souls with the Holy Spirit and our hearts with the peace of Christ Jesus.

Oh Lord, help us to become servants. Take our minds and think through them, take our lips and speak through them, and take our hearts and set them on fire!

41
Unintended Consequences

By Larry Welke

"I was in prison and you visited me" (Matthew 25:36c).

I work with inner-city youth, teaching them how to do video storytelling for business and personal communication. This past semester, my best student was a sixteen-year-old who picked up the ability to write a good story, add dialogue, build in suspense and intrigue in the most ordinary plot, and describe his protagonist in believable detail. I didn't teach him all that; he was a natural. He had God-given talent.

In the spring he missed a few classes halfway through videotaping one of his stories. That was unusual enough to cause a call to his mother to find out what was happening. After several attempts I finally reached her, only to hear an explanation I didn't want to hear. He was in the Marion County jail.

He'd been there for a month, having been picked up by the police along with three of his friends for having broken into a stranger's house. They robbed the only occupant and, after a scuffle, they shot him dead.

I didn't want to believe it. I thought a sixteen-year-old couldn't do such a thing —certainly not this sixteen-year-old. It's near impossible to call a jail inmate, so I wrote him a letter expressing my concern, not passing judgment on anything I'd heard, and offering my prayers and whatever support was possible.

Within two days he wrote back, thanking me for the prayers, expressing his fears and the uncertainty as to what he thought would happen to him. He said he was involved in the robbery but not the murder, and he was praying the court-appointed lawyer was going to be a good one. I wrote back saying I couldn't afford to hire an attorney, but I would volunteer to raise money to pay for one if his family could find one.

They did. The new lawyer visited him in the jail and reported back that my student had been charged as an accomplice and would probably spend some extended time in prison. The most a lawyer could do, he said, was possibly minimize the sentence but even that would be expensive because of it being a complex case—multiple defendants, multiple charges, etc.

I wrote another letter, explaining the situation as bluntly and honestly as I knew how, and closed saying I would attend his trial and would follow through with visits and letters. And prayers.

And I will. He made a mistake, and he knows there is a price to pay. If I can keep him writing stories and praying, he'll lose a couple of years of freedom but at least he won't lose his life.

Oh God, we ask your forgiveness of us when we fail you and harm others. May every mistake become an opportunity for spiritual growth. Amen.

42
United Christmas Service

By Terry Corman

"While they were there, the time came for her to deliver her child. And she gave birth to her firstborn son and wrapped him in bands of cloth, and laid him in a manger, because there was no place for them in the inn"
(Luke 2:6-7).

While driving together to work one December morning and listening to the radio, my wife and I heard a public service announcement asking for donations to United Christmas Service. Later that same day, she came to me and said she could not get the announcement out of her mind, and that she felt we had to do something immediately. A quick call to the United Christmas Service office that afternoon yielded a simple answer to the question as to what we could do at that late date in December. The answer was, "Write a check." My wife, Sally, got in her car and dropped off a check.

But the pull of United Christmas Service did not go away after writing a check, and we found ourselves wanting to do more for the following year. As the next season came around, we asked for and were assigned a family that we could "adopt" and give gifts to directly. The discussion around our adopted Christmas Service family came up at one of our own family dinners, and both of my daughter's-in-law asked to be a part of our giving as well.

As Christmas approached we were assigned our family, and we set up a time to meet with a mother of two young girls as she was moving into a new apartment. When we arrived at our meeting, we entered an apartment that had a blanket. That was it. One blanket, nothing else. The two beautiful young girls slept on the floor with the blanket, and the mother slept on the floor with nothing.

My wife and two daughters-in-law explained to the young mother that they would be back, and soon. Several families showed up at that empty apartment at the appointed time as Christmas approached. An outpouring of love and generosity was loaded into three trucks, and I will never forget as the moments passed, as an empty apartment became one filled with love and compassion and sofas, chairs and lamps, dishes and glasses, every kitchen appliance, bedding, clothes to fill closets, a television, a radio, and yes, a Christmas tree and presents galore. It was a complete makeover, from literally nothing to virtually everything.

It was a joyous occasion for every one of us, my grandchildren got to see what giving is all about, and several families got to come together for one special prayer around that Christmas tree. We had been called to be faithful to those with the greatest need.

Oh God, thank you for those with compassionate hearts and who share with people in need, not only at Christmas but throughout the year. Amen.

43
Voice of the Heart

By Minnietta Millard

"Of this gospel I have become a servant according to the gift of God's grace that was given to me by the working of his power. Although I am the very least of all the saints, this grace was given to me to bring to the Gentiles the news of the boundless riches of Christ, and to make everyone see what is the plan of the mystery hidden for ages in God who created all things; so that through the church the wisdom of God in its rich variety might now be made known to the rulers and authorities in the heavenly places" (Ephesians 3:7-10).

As is true with a great many people, I find it necessary to make choices about which responsibilities I accept and which I turn down. I've learned to go inward and get in touch with my feelings. If I have positive feeling, I say "yes." If there is a begrudged feeling or negative reaction, I say "no."

When asked by the University of Indianapolis (UIndy) to work on the Bridge Building Committee for Mar Elias, a school where Jews, Christians, Muslims and Druze study together in peace in Northern Galilee, I went to my inner soul for discernment. It was there that I found an excitement brewing. As a result I said "yes" to the task.

My first step was introducing my friends from the church to the school. The openness I experienced from church members was joyous! It was as if people were just waiting to get involved with a project that inspired them. And the contributions continue to grow as people in the church find a part of their inner soul responding to the needs of these students halfway around the world.

At least two dozen church members have flown to Israel and visited the Mar Elias campus, where they were touched to the core of their hearts with the peace that emanated from the students, faculty, and facilities. One couple from the church has even spent several semesters in residence at the college to teach English and mathematics, and to more securely build the bridge between the two universities.

There is no end to what God can do through members of our church communities when each of us listens to the "voice of the heart" within us. Our church communities have an endless supply of energy and passion for reaching out to the needs of the world when educated about ways to make it happen. People are just waiting to be asked for a project that resonates with their soul. And then God's love becomes real through the hands, time, and resources of Christ's people.

With Paul, Oh God, may we feel the passion in our hearts that will lead us to serve. Amen.

44
Water and Living Water

By Michael J. Coyner

"Jesus answered her, 'If you knew the gift of God, and who it is that is saying to you, "Give me a drink," you would have asked him, and he would have given you living water'" (John 4:10).

During a Bishops meeting in Maputo, Mozambique, my wife Marsha and I visited a new congregation. We traveled to the edge of Maputo, to a very poor area, down several dirt roads, and finally came to the location of the Bispo Escrivao Zumguze Igreja Metodist a Unida Em Mozambique, which is a new church start named for a previous bishop (Bishop Zumguze). The only enclosed structure for this new church was a concrete slab with bamboo walls, and they had outgrown that facility, so worship that Sunday was literally conducted under two trees and a tarp. The church was established in 2001 but already had 508 members, and it was easy to see why. Such music! Such spirit! Such hospitality! And such passion for reaching people for Christ.

I was especially impressed that they spent their early funds to provide a well on their land to give free water to the people of the surrounding poor neighborhood. Rather than spend their first money on themselves, on their own building, they have focused upon providing water—indeed Living Water—to their community.

The church is led by the president of the congregation, a layman named Pedro, and by their pastor, a young woman named Berta. They had a large adult choir, a youth choir, and lots of well-behaved children seated on bamboo mats on the ground. New members were received that Sunday, and they were immediately assigned to the "local congregations" in various neighborhoods, which function along the lines of the old Methodist Class meeting to train new converts into discipleship. Food was provided and everyone was fed, including those too poor to bring their own food. Perhaps the most enthusiastic part of the service was the offering, or I should say the offerings. The first offering was given by those who wanted to declare publicly that they were tithing. Then individuals came and gave offerings from each of the local churches, or classes. Then we gave our offerings, which prompted a most exuberant additional offering by everyone as people came forward to give again. Each offering was full of music, people dancing forward to give, and a total sense of what the Scriptures mean by "God loves a cheerful giver" (2 Corinthians 9:7).

I reflected later that day on the words of a favorite hymn, "God of Grace and God of Glory," which confesses that we are "rich in things and poor in soul." In the Bispo Zumguze church that Sunday, I witnessed people who were poor in things but very rich in soul. I found myself wondering how many of our churches in the U.S. would be content to worship under two trees and a tarp. Now, don't get me wrong, the Bispo Zumguze has plans to build a facility as soon as they can raise the funds. There is nothing inherently wrong with having church facilities. But there is something refreshing about the joy of having church under two trees and a tarp. Maybe it is what helped them to offer both water and Living Water to their community.

Lord, forgive us when we are "rich in things and poor in soul." Help us to serve You by offering both water and Living Water to our communities. Amen.

45
Winnie

By Nancy Spohn

"And the king will answer them, 'Truly I tell you, just as you did it to one of the least of these who are members of my family, you did it to me'"
(Matthew 25:40).

I met Winnie in the fall. She was from Bulawayo, Zimbabwe; her husband had been killed four years earlier in a hit-and-run accident. In Zimbabwe, when a man dies, all of his debts become due. He had just borrowed money to start a new business. In order to comply with the law, Winnie and her four children lost their house, their car, and all their possessions. They were literally walking the streets.

Winnie had hurt her back trying to carry vegetables to feed her family. She had received back surgery after lying in the hospital for six months, and she was in more pain than before the surgery. She was brought to the United States by her sister, who was in the Zimbabwe military but stationed here for a nursing course. Winnie's sister hoped she could find physical therapy here to help Winnie recover.

I met Winnie through the Nunery family, who had just lost their house due to a fire. Winnie was working for them in order to salvage some of the burned items. She was living in the basement of the Nunery rental house, and the moment I saw her I realized her despair.

I worked very hard to help her get a driver's license and a Social Security number, and started on the long route to get her a green card so she would be legal. I knew very little about immigration requirements, but I realized she was in a rowboat rowing by herself, and that she and her four children were going to sink if someone didn't help them. God put her and her family securely in my heart.

I was able to secure a scholarship to a technical school for her second son, Challenge, and he came to the United States on an academic visa. He lived with us for four years and graduated from ITT Tech. Winnie lived with us for six months until she moved into an apartment. We were able to get her other two sons to Canada on a refugee status the day before September 11, 2001. They have received their citizenship from Canada, and one is now living in Indianapolis; the other should be moving here soon.

Winnie joined St. Luke's UMC seven years ago and never misses church. She is also working for St. Luke's and pursuing her green card. I sent out a letter asking for financial help from St. Luke's members seven years ago, and a nice fund was raised to help her family. She loves the members of St. Luke's.

Winnie's family has become like my own. Our friendship has brought us both closer to God. She still has one daughter and a granddaughter in Zimbabwe, and we pray every day that somehow, some way we will be able to bring them to the U.S. so the whole family can live in America where they will be safe. They only want to be able to work and be together as a family, which is not possible in the current corrupt political climate of Zimbabwe.

Oh God, we pray for people who have to leave their homes because of war or political unrest. May they always find open arms and loving spirits to welcome them. Amen.

46
Words on Pieces of Wood

By Adolf Hansen

"The blessing of the Lord be upon you! We bless you in the name of the Lord!"
(Psalm 129:8).

"Would you like to buy a 2 x 4? They're $10 each." These were the words spoken on that spring Sunday morning at the main entrance to the sanctuary. They were repeated over and over again, both before and after each of the services at the church.

As individuals, couples, and families stopped to buy one, two, or more of the 2 x 4's, they were invited to take one of the markers and write a blessing, a prayer, or a wish, large enough for anyone to read. They were also told that what they wrote should be directed to the family who would live in the Habitat for Humanity house that members of the church were going to build.

The words were so wonderful! One said, "Bless this house, O Lord." Another, "May you sense God's presence here." Still another, "We will remember to pray for you." And so many more. "May love fill this home." "May joy be heard in every room." "May hope be felt in every heart."

Almost everyone coming to church that morning was aware of what was going on. The side entrance as well as the front entrance had stacks and stacks of lumber, each piece eight feet long. As a 2 x 4 was purchased, and the words were written, they were leaned up against the walls for everyone to see.

It was a very successful morning. Hundreds of 2 x 4's were sold. But that was not the end of the project. It was only the beginning. For those words on pieces of wood showed up over and over again as members of the congregation loaded the lumber on to a truck, unloaded it at the site of the build, and used it to erect walls in the house.

Each of these steps led people to read and reread what had been written. But the most meaningful part of this process was when the future homeowner came into the house, greeted several of us who were working there, and started reading the words. She was quiet as she moved from one 2 x 4 to another, pausing to read and then reflect—sometimes having to ask for help to decipher some of the handwriting. Some words were read aloud; others in silence. And then the mother who was going to live in the house, with tears welling up in her eyes, said, "These words make me feel so good. And to think that they are going to be all around me, even when they are all covered up. My, oh my."

We paused, with teary eyes as well, as we hugged, as we talked, and as we walked and read again the words on pieces of wood.

Gracious God, we share your blessings with others and, when we do, we are blessed ourselves. Help us to keep on doing this—as often as we can. Amen.

47
Chili and Children in Need

By Steve Badger

"The Kingdom of Heaven is like a mustard seed that someone took and sowed in his field; it is the smallest of all the seeds, but when it has grown it is the greatest of shrubs and becomes a tree, so that the birds of the air come and make nests in its branches" (Matthew 13:31-32).

When our church offered us the opportunity to participate in the "pay it forward" project, I truly felt inspired to make the most of the opportunity and I derived great satisfaction from the effort.

I used the $25 to host a chili lunch for my colleagues at work. In exchange for providing lunch, I asked each of them to make a small contribution in an amount proportionate to what they would pay for a modest lunch at a restaurant. The proceeds would go to Kids' Voice, a local charity that, among other things, supports and provides Guardians Ad Litem for children in CHINS (Child In Need of Services) and divorce cases.

When I totaled my receipts for the chili and accessories, I had spent $25.27. Ten people from my office attended the luncheon, which raised $100. The project inspired me to match those cash contributions. So I sent a check to Kids' Voice for $200, an eightfold increase from the $25 in "seed money."

Oh God, we are humbled and grateful when we see how you take our small efforts and multiply them in ways we could not have imagined. Help us to do whatever we can to serve someone else because we know you use our small efforts to create large blessings. In Christ's name. Amen.

(For more information, see http://www.kidsvoicein.org/)

48
Paying It Forward

By Amanda Snobarger

"Each of you must give as you have made up your mind, not reluctantly or under compulsion, for God loves a cheerful giver. And God is able to provide you with every blessing in abundance, so that by always having enough of everything you may share abundantly in every good work" (2 Corinthians 9:7-8).

I was not a member of church, but I attended pretty regularly and was in attendance the day that the sermon topic was "Pay it Forward." I had seen the movie a few years ago and thought it was very touching and also viewed the Oprah show in which she gave the audience members money to "pay it forward." I felt that this was an excellent idea and decided to take part.

I debated how I should utilize this money so that it would impact someone directly and hopefully many more indirectly. After tossing around some different ideas, I finally opted to use this money for a cause that is very important to me.

For the last few years I have worked as a school counselor. When I left my school this past September to take a new position, it was very difficult to say good-bye to some students with whom I worked very closely. Several of these young students had faced many hardships in their lifetime. Some often did not have a reason to strive academically or to become involved at school, and others did not feel as if they were cared for or that they were important. While it was difficult to see all of this, it was very rewarding when I knew that I was making a difference in the lives of these young adolescents. I wanted the students to know that they inspired me and I wanted to encourage them to give back to those who inspired them.

I chose to give the $25 and a bit extra to a few of my previous students, along with a letter. The letter indicated that they had in some way touched my life as I saw them overcome obstacles and do some wonderful things. I explained that I was giving them this letter and money because they were inspiring to me, and I wanted to encourage them to give a token of appreciation or gratitude to a person who touched their life in some way. I suggested that perhaps with the holidays approaching they could each thank the person who helped them to be the strong people they are today. I went on to encourage them to continue the idea of paying it forward.

One of my letters was sent to a student who had a mother who worked four jobs to provide for her daughters. I have never seen a work ethic like this. Last year we helped this mother to be able to have a nice Christmas dinner and some gifts for her two daughters. I will never forget how thankful this mother or my student was. I have never seen anyone express their appreciation as this mother and daughter did. It was inspiring.

I'm so grateful for the opportunity to pay it forward.

Oh God, we pray for those who struggle to overcome hardship and difficulty in their lives. Use our prayers, love, and compassionate actions to be a sign of hope for all persons in need of hope. In Christ's name. Amen.

49
The Snoezelen Room

By Mike Musa

"Honor your father and your mother, as the Lord your God commanded you, so that your days may be long and that it may go well with you in the land that the Lord your God is giving you" (Deuteronomy 5:16).

The following is part of a solicitation letter that we sent to family and friends as part of our participation in the church's Pay It Forward campaign:

October 26

Dear friends and family,

"At a recent church service, our minister announced that an anonymous donor had arranged for envelopes containing $25 in cash to be available at the end of the service to anyone who wanted them. Needless to say, there was a catch, and that was to use the $25 as seed money to be multiplied and applied towards a good cause, preferably consistent with our church's current theme of inter-generational service.

Well, we took the bait. We decided to use the $25 to buy 61 stamps to solicit 61 donations of $25 (where you come into the picture) with the proceeds going to benefit Westminster Village North's secured memory care units. Westminster Village North is a wonderful, not-for-profit continuum care retirement community that has been Mike's parents' home since January. It encompasses independent living, assisted living, and nursing care facilities. Within the assisted living and nursing care facilities there are separate "secured" memory care units for residents afflicted with advanced dementia.

As many of you know, Mike's dad was diagnosed with Alzheimer's disease; the last year has provided us an unsolicited crash course on Alzheimer's and other dementia-related conditions and on the heavy toll placed on both patients and families by these awful and insidious illnesses.

Your contribution will go towards the building of a "Snoezelen Room" inside the secured assisted living memory care unit. Snoezelen rooms provide sensory therapy that has been found to be helpful in managing and soothing the agitation and confusion experienced by many afflicted with dementia. This initiative is being funded by private donations outside the normal Westminster Village North budgeting process.

Earlier in the week a dementia caregiver support group that meets at Westminster heard of our effort and decided to also engage in raising funds for the room. In fact, one generous resident offered to match up to $1,000 raised by that group. With any luck the original $25 gift will be multiplied many times over and for a good cause indeed."

Well, the outcome from our letter to friends and family has been more than gratifying. As of late November we have received 38 contributions adding up to $2,300!! Further, an Alzheimer's support group that meets at Westminster got wind of our effort and decided to join in and has raised $1,200. And then the Westminster Village community at large got involved and has committed $5,600 to the cause.

Remarkably, the original, anonymous $25 cash donation has grown to $9,100! Not a penny of this would have been raised without the original $25 in cash as that served as the genesis for the project. The Westminster Village community is very excited about this project and has established a goal of raising a total of $20,000 to adequately equip the Snoezelen room. There is now no question that this room will soon go from Westminster's "wish list" to reality, and based on the enthusiasm I've observed I am confident that the Westminster community will figure out a way to raise the entire $20,000 they have targeted.

The Snoezelen Room

I am writing this right before Thanksgiving and I assure you that among the many things Deb and I will be thankful for this year will be the spirit of caring and generosity represented by those who have participated in this effort—for the original anonymous donor of the $25—and for those of you at St. Luke's that made this happen.

Oh God, we thank you for our parents and for the ways they cared for us when we were younger. Now, may we express that same compassion when we care for our parents in their times of need. In Christ's name. Amen.

50
It's Raining Wheelchairs

By Debbie Shook

"Then some people came, bringing to him a paralyzed man, carried by four of them. And when they could not bring him to Jesus because of the crowd, they removed the roof above him and after having dug through it, they let down the mat on which the paralytic lay. When Jesus saw their faith, he said to the paralytic, "Son your sins are forgiven" (Mark 2:3-5).

On the Sunday we all received our $25 Pay It Forward seed money, I sent an e-mail to close friends about my idea to benefit the ALS Association of Indiana. ALS, or as it is commonly known, Lou Gehrig's Disease, is a devastating and debilitating neurological condition which destroys the victim's muscles, one muscle at a time. Persons with this condition have a life expectancy of from two to five years. ALS does not affect the mind, only the body. It is always terminal.

My husband Neil suffered with this disease for seven-and-a-half years. Our two sons were eleven and thirteen when their Dad was diagnosed with ALS. We all suffered tremendously during his decline. Neil passed away with our family and close friends at his bedside in our home on the last day of June, 2003.

ALS patients' conditions vary in where it strikes first, but all of them lose the ability to use their limbs, one limb at a time. In addition to the many, many emotional and physical struggles families of these patients suffer, the financial burden of buying equipment to assist their loved one is often overwhelming. In direct response to that need, the ALS Association of Indiana has a loan closet which assists families in decreasing that financial burden.

I simply asked my friends to match, more or less, my $25 so that we could purchase a few items for the ALS closet. After speaking with the executive director of the ALS Association here in Indianapolis, she advised they needed lightweight transport wheelchairs and rolling walkers with brakes. These items are loaned to the families and then returned to the ALS closet for use by other families once their loved one has passed away or can no longer use them.

After receiving a few pledges, I went to the bank to open a special "ALS Closet" account. The bank manager gave us a free account, free checks, and made a donation of $25 to the account. Just one more example of how paying it forward can create a ripple effect of helping others.

Although my goal was simply to buy two, maybe three items for the closet, my dear friends donated enough money for us to purchase three wheelchairs and four walkers. Walgreens drug store offered these items at a sale price two weeks into our campaign. Upon explaining our Pay it Forward campaign to the store manager, Walgreens donated an additional wheelchair!

My son Ryan delivered these items to the ALS closet in Indianapolis, and one of the walkers was loaned out that afternoon to a family in need. The addition of four wheelchairs and four walkers to the ALS closet was a gift for those families, and we are blessed that we were able to help.

Oh God, thank you for the faith, love and commitment of those who care for persons with life-debilitating illnesses. Surround them all with your comforting strength and your healing power. In Christ's name. Amen.

51
School #20

By Jody Wyss-Treadwell

"Then little children were being brought to him in order that he might lay his hands on them and pray. The disciples spoke sternly to those who brought them; but Jesus said: 'Let the little children come to me, and do not stop them; for it is to such as these that the kingdom of heaven belongs.' And he laid his hands on them and went on his way" (Matthew 19: 13-15).

The following letter was written by a teacher at Indianapolis Public School #20, an inner-city school that the people of our church reached out to and became partners with in 2006. She wrote the following note to the our congregation:

"My sincere thanks . . . for the many notes throughout the year from a wonderful lady, whom I do not even believe I have had the opportunity nor the pleasure to meet, made some of our most difficult days seem not quite so difficult after all. It is a moment of joy to find a kind word and a pleasant thought in my mailbox of a morning before the start of a school day.

"For all of the people who sent material, costumes, and circus banners, you were more than generous. The children felt so proud of their accomplishments. They walked a little taller in their costumes; they tumbled and juggled like none better for their age. When we practiced juggling in the room with scarves it looked like a rainbow of color had exploded. Scarves were flying everywhere and so was the laughter and joy from the children.

"Thank you for the many books we received throughout the year for the children to keep as their very own. It is a pleasure and a sense of satisfaction to see a student reading his or her book as they walk in line down the hall, so intent on what they are reading that they can't put it down.

"To all of the volunteers who tirelessly worked with our children as tutors and mentors, thank you. The joy you gave to those children will never be known, but in our hearts we know you made a difference. To see a familiar face week after week is such a source of strength and affirmation to our children. Consistency is what they crave most and need the most to build a stronger, self-disciplined attitude from within their very being. You set the example for them to follow.

"I know I am missing so many wonderful things you provided for the children of our school. Personally, I was not involved in every activity that had the loving hands of a St. Luke's volunteer guiding it to success. But as a member of the faculty, I want you to know that it is always noticed.

"We all remain dedicated to the positive influences each of us tries to make upon the lives of our students . . . May God continue to bless the St. Luke's family."

Oh God, we pray for all teachers and their students. We thank you for educators who dedicate their time and talent to inspiring the next generation and for those who support them in their efforts. In Christ's name. Amen.

52

Two Dreamers, Two Years and Ten Thousand Volunteers Later...

By Bob Zehr

"What good is it, my brothers and sisters, if you say you have faith but do not have works? Can faith save you? If a brother or sister is naked and lacks daily food, and one of you says to them, 'Go in peace; keep warm and eat your fill,' and yet you do not supply their bodily needs, what is the good of that? So faith by itself, if it has no works is dead" (James 2:14-17).

Over the past twenty years, Ken Hollis has participated in over ninety work projects, but when he, Al Dalton, and others from the St. Luke's mission team arrived in D'Iberville, Mississippi to see where we could help, it was obvious that more than a one-week work project would be required. The damage from Hurricane Katrina was unimaginable.

Ken and Al were taken on a special tour behind the emergency lines by the United Methodist Committee on Relief (UMCOR) team when they convinced the relief agency that St. Luke's could help provide leadership in a bigger way. The local District Superintendent introduced them to the pastor of Heritage UMC, Dave Cumbest, who had already mobilized his congregation in the relief efforts. The parking lot of the church had become a major distribution center for bottled water, food and emergency supplies, and the congregation had quickly taken on the responsibility for helping its members and neighbors through this crisis. The church was getting daily calls from volunteers around the country looking for ways to help.

Rev. Cumbest was slightly skeptical about the plan that Al and Ken presented, but when they suggested building a volunteer center that could house fifty people and said that they would help raise the money to build it, Dave gave his enthusiastic blessing. During the Lenten season, our congregation gave over $50,000 to be combined with another $100,000 from other churches in the Indiana conferences, and work began on thirty-five-hundred-square-foot building. Teams from St. Luke's and other Indiana churches descended upon the Heritage church property, often sleeping on pews in the sanctuary or in the back of pickup trucks. Six weeks later, the dormitory was ready for occupancy.

Since Heritage Church began to serve as a disaster relief center, just days after Hurricane Katrina, over forty-five-thousand volunteers from around the country have worked through the volunteer coordinators of this small three-hundred-member church, including nearly ten-thousand volunteers who have enjoyed the "comforts" of the center that grew from the idea that Ken and Al launched that day. These volunteers have helped over seven hundred families return to their homes, yet there are still many that need help.

Can individuals make a difference in the efforts to provide comfort and care in the wake of the biggest natural disaster to ever hit our country? Ken Hollis and Al Dalton are perfect examples of what we as individuals can do when we reach out with compassion and determination to make a difference.

Oh God, thank you for those who put their faith into action by using their skills and commitment to provide food, water, clothing and shelter to those who have been beaten and battered by the storms of life. In Christ's name. Amen.

TOGETHER IN MINISTRY EVERYDAY

52 Devotions

Other Resources for
Together in Ministry Everyday

T.I.M.E. Workbook (9780687653287)
T.I.M.E. 52 Devotions (9780687653683)
T.I.M.E. DVD (9780687653485)
T.I.M.E. Planning Kit (9780687653584)